D1472337

TELEVISION'S IMAGEABLE INFLUENCES

The Self-Perceptions of Young African-Americans

Camille O. Cosby, Ed.D.

UNIVERSITY PRESS OF AMERICA

Lanham • New York • London

University Press of America,® Inc.

4720 Boston Way
Lanham, Maryland 20706

3 Henrietta Street
London WC2E 8LU England

Cover illustration by
Erika R. Cosby, M.F.A.
and
Edited by
Wellington Y. Chiu, Ph.D.

Library of Congress Cataloging-in-Publication Data

Cosby, Camille O. (Camille Olivia).
Television's imageable influences : the self-perceptions of young
African-Americans / Camille O. Cosby.
p.   cm.
Includes bibliographical references and index.
1. Afro-American youth—Attitudes.   2. Television broadcasting—
Social aspects—United States.   3. Afro-Americans in television.
4. Public opinion—United States.   I. Title.
E185.86.C58215   1993
305.23'08996073—dc20   94–9258 CIP

ISBN 0–8191–9521–9 (cloth : alk. paper)

∞™ The paper used in this publication meets the minimum requirements of
American National Standard for Information Sciences—Permanence
of Paper for Printed Library Materials, ANSI Z39.48–1984.

To

The millions of young adult African-Americans,
who, as change agents, will impact positive
transformational African-American
imageries on television.

CONTENTS

Preface

Acknowledgments

List of Tables

List of Figures

Author's Note

PREFACE

TELEVISION'S IMAGEABLE INFLUENCES: THE SELF-PERCEPTIONS OF YOUNG AFRICAN-AMERICANS

The purpose of the study was to determine the possible influence of particular television imageries of African-Americans on the self-perceptions of selected young adult African-Americans, ages eighteen to twenty-five. The focus of the study was on specific aspects of self that are addressed by particular television imageries of African-Americans and the possible influences that particular television imageries have on self-perceptions of selected young adult African-Americans.

For the design of the study, a qualitative methodology was deemed most useful. Three African-American judges participated in the study: a social psychologist, an anthropologist, and a psychiatrist. The judges were asked to identify and analyze the positive and/or negative imageries that they thought may influence the self-concept of African-American young adults. Thus, the judges provided data for the study.

Additionally, in-depth interviewing was determined to be the most useful method for gathering data from ten young adult African-Americans. The interview sessions were conducted in 1991 and included the viewing of nineteen episodes of a popular television show featuring African-American actors/actresses. Afterwards, the interviewees were asked to express their perceptions of the African-American television imageries.

Profiles of the interviewees were established from a personal history form, and data from the interviews were analyzed.

The judges' data explain that the television images are likely to have negative influences on self-perceptions of the young African-American viewers. Moreover, the judges overwhelmingly agreed that degrading stereotypes are the major likely influences on self.

Thirty hours of interviews with ten African-American adults revealed that the subjects differed in their perceptions of the possible influence of the television programming on their self-perceptions. Although differences in perceptions existed, only one respondent perceived all television episodes to have negative influences, except for the hybrids. Many of the episodes were viewed as having the potential for positive and negative influences. The judges perceived the television imageries to be negative. Yet the young African-Americans who were interviewed tended to see the same imagery as being positive. This difference in perception among different generations of African-Americans may be attributed to thoughts about humor and ridicule. Also, the limited life experiences of those being interviewed may influence their critical consciousness and thus contribute to the tendency to be more tolerant of the possible negative impact the images may have on their views of themselves.

The television industry must join the effort to make education a more positive and powerful means for equality in our democracy.

ACKNOWLEDGMENTS

I dedicate this book and extend my deepest gratitude to those who helped me travel this far with my educational pursuits. Foremost, to William H. Cosby, Jr., who is my friend, partner and loving, lovable husband. Also, I respect him because his career has been characterized by laborious and diligent efforts and commitments to creating, producing, and projecting positive television imageries of African-Americans, despite many obstacles.

• To my daughter, Ensa, who sketched and copied papers for the book; to my youngest daughter, Evin, who lived without me for three days per week for two years; to my daughter and son, Erika and Ennis, respectively, for being principal supporters.

• To Dr. Norma Jean Anderson, Chairperson of my Committee, who is the consummate educator because of her devotion to her students, regardless of their religion, color, or sex; to Dr. Robert L. Sinclair, my Committee Member, who spent countless hours with me offering suggestions to improve my book; to Dr. Diane Flaherty and Dr. Randolph W. Bromery, my other Committee Members, who gave me expert and sincere guidance.

• To my brother, Eric M. Hanks, who taught me statistical skills; to Sondra Pugh, for typing my numerous book drafts and serving as my assistant during the interviewees' sessions at New York City's Apollo Theatre; to Percy Sutton, who allowed me to use the Apollo Theatre for conducting interviews; to Besida Tonwe, who was my principal researcher; to Dr. Steve Goldberg, for giving instructions on library research; and to Wellington and Eli Chiu, for their technological assistance.

• To Christine Philpot, Dr. David Driskell, Dr. John Henrik Clarke, Norman Brokaw, Barry Stich, Rosemary O'Brien, David Brokaw, Beverly Grymes Hemmings, Joel

Brokaw, Dr. C. Boyd James, Charlayne Hunter-Gault, and Gary Grossman, for contributing multitudinous historical documents, films, and verbal information to aid the study.

• To Minnie Goka, Karen Ellis, and Arvilla F. Isley, for selecting the ten young African-American adult participants for the study; to Clarence Beverly and Allison Thomson, for providing transportation to and from the University of Massachusetts; and to Tammy Echols-Howell, Shirley Adcock, Josephine Chambers, Edith Bell, Elham Yassin, and John Ste. Marthe, for being enthusiastic supporters.

• To my assistant, Helena Keohane, who was responsible for all logistical arrangements and typing letters to some of the participants in the study. Also, I dedicate the body of work to Nancy Kaminski, an invaluable organizer, who typed this book.

• To Leroy, Keri, John, Ahmed, Elizabeth, Barbara, Lisa, Thelma, David, and Gordon, for participating in the *study* and for enlightening me about young people's thoughts and ideas pertaining to television imageries.

• To Dr. Kenneth B. Clark, Dr. Johnnetta B. Cole, and Dr. Alvin F. Poussaint, for presenting their professional analyses which were of great worth to the study.

• To Gladys E. Rodgers, Carolyn W. Lewis, and Gloria Foster, for being my very special friends.

• Finally, to my parents, Guy A. Hanks, Sr., and Catherine C. Hanks, who continued the family tradition of pursuing educational opportunities and social and political justice, despite the obstacles that derive from the United States of America's institutional racism. Moreover, I dedicate this to my African foremothers and forefathers, for paving the way for me and the earth's people.

List of Tables

List of Figures

AUTHOR'S NOTE

The original study document embodied five photographs that portrayed African-American actors/actresses as they were seen on film. Some photographs were from *Gone With the Wind*, a David O. Selznick Production, featuring Hattie McDaniel and *The Country Chairman*, a Fox Film Production, featuring Stepin Fetchit.

However, when I sought permission to use the photographs for this book, I was required by some of the current owners of the photographs to sign agreements that would in effect have me warrantee that the picture, any person connected with the production of the picture or depicted therein would not be used in any derogatory way.

Since the photographs of the African-American actors/actresses are derogatory in their essence due to the negative stereotypical depictions, I did not sign the agreements. Thus the photographs were not used in this book.

Camille O. Cosby
July 1993

I

INTRODUCTION

STATEMENT OF THE PROBLEM

In 1620, the welfare program for America's controlling strata was established, and the enslavement of millions of African people would take place for the next two centuries. Africans soon became the commodities and unpaid laborers for the Portuguese, Spanish, British, Dutch, French, and a few other European groups of people (*Ebony Magazine* Editors, 1971). Now, at the end of the twentieth century, many of America's estimated thirty million African-blooded people are still functioning as commodities and as cheap labor for the controlling strata. Many African-Americans are low-paid builders, bridge builders, factory workers, garment workers, domestic workers, agricultural laborers, janitors, and soldiers for the American descendants of the Portuguese, Spanish, British, Dutch, French, and other European-Americans.

However, as African-Americans are trying to form coalitions and strategize offensive tactics to gain and maintain their civil rights, the controlling strata are increasingly replacing the low-paid African-American laborers with Central American, Asian, South American, and Eastern European low-paid laborers. Thus, the formerly low-paid African-American worker becomes unemployed, poorer, and more powerless.

Throughout the history of America, the controlling strata created and encouraged a growing gap between themselves and the citizenry of African ancestry. Exclusionary practices relating to health, employment, housing, and education for African-Americans permeate throughout American society. A major mark of discrimination, in fact, the purpose of discrimination, is to keep the African-American populace far away from the benefits of health, housing, education, and the anticipation of a better life. This behavior by the controlling strata is the poverty of unselfishness. Greed makes the controlling strata the dollar beneficiaries of what are presently their welfare programs: the numerous lucrative military and corporate umbrella entities and their respective subsidiaries.

Yet, there is another poverty – the poverty of the truth relative to distortions that exist in the midst of millions of television and other media pictures – which frequently characterize African-Americans. Even *Webster's Dictionary* (1976) defines black as "soiled with dirt; dirty; outrageously wicked; deserving unmitigated condemnation; expressing or indicating disgrace, dishonor, discredit, or guilt; and dark in comparison to the average complexion of a group." Additionally, the controlling strata have instituted and propagandized words to describe and apply to African-Americans. Terms such as out-group, minority, third-world, disadvantaged, criminal, low-life, poor, drugs, and incarceration seem to persist. Unfortunately, some African-Americans are using these words to convey their self-images to others.

The practices of media distortion may affect the self-esteem of young African-Americans in negative ways. Self-image and self-esteem relate to perceptions of one's group (Norton, 1983). If one has a low level of self-esteem, then one will not likely succeed; one will not likely self-actualize or self-affirm. Hence, one may not become self-empowered.

There has been a systematic exclusion of positive images of African-Americans in mainstream art, radio, school textbooks, newspapers, history books, magazines, television, movies, videos, and other forms of media. If African-Americans do not self-define, then they are being described too often by 'others' through 'others' perceptions. Being described only by 'others' can be ubiquitously destructive for African-Americans or any people.

John Henry Clarke (1990), Professor Emeritus of African Studies, noted that:

> *African people can have a Golden Age or another*
> *Age of Continued Despair depending on how they*
> *view themselves in relationship to the totality of*

> *history and its ironies. The cruelest thing slavery and colonialism did to the Africans was to destroy their memory of what they were before foreign contact.*

Dr. Clarke's statement elicits a crucial question: If African-Americans do not know their history because of distortions and exclusions of African-American history in America's history books and other forms of media, then how can African-Americans define themselves?

Despite the controlling strata's practices of health, political, social, historical, and educational exclusion, African-Americans have managed to achieve many victories. Despite the powers that move against them, many African-Americans have accomplished the arduous feat of forcing the controlling strata to include egalitarian principles by amendments to America's Constitution. After all, the writers of the Constitution excluded America's African-blooded people from the pages of the Constitution. Through marches and protests, African-Americans have incessantly reminded the American citizenry of the principles of a true democratic society and the meaning of humanitarianism.

One of the controlling strata's most powerful tools that markets imageries and definitions of African-Americans is television. Approximately ninety-eight percent of American homes have television sets. Thus, the imageries that are perpetuated on television are likely to be powerful and persuasive for all viewers. O'Connor (1991) stated:

> *Television is a business and must be concerned with turning a profit. But television is no ordinary business. Its very prevalence in the lives of most citizens makes the medium the dominant force of society. Anyone who has ever watched television with a child knows firsthand how frighteningly influential the small screen can be in suggesting not only what to buy but also how to behave and speak and, indeed, what to think.*

To understand the power of television, one must be knowledgeable about the entities that control television programming. Lee and Solomon (1990) wrote:

> *TV affects the thinking and behavior of more people in our society than any other information technology. . . . The major TV networks, which continue to capture the lion's share of viewers and revenue, have also succumbed to the forces of merger and consolidation. In the mid-1980s, as a result of eased ownership, rules drafted by Reagan's FCC, the Big Three came under new management even less interested in creative broadcasting than in harnessing the bottom line. ABC fell to Cap Cities, a wealthy but unimpressive news chain. Shortly thereafter, General Electric, a leading military contractor and union buster, gobbled up NBC. Lawrence Tisch, a hardnosed hotel and tobacco tycoon, grabbed the reins at CBS after it barely survived a couple of hostile takeover attempts. With few exceptions, cable TV serves up imitative programming hardly different from the major networks. Most cable systems are owned by companies that already control other media. The parent firms of ABC and NBC, for example, have big investments in cable.*

Since so few entities own and control the television industry, these entities may have a monopoly on socializing and conditioning human perceptions. If this socialization is distorted, it then becomes a powerful tool for perpetuating negative images of African-Americans.

In television, as in all forms of media, most African-Americans do not control the content, the acting, nor the productions of their work. Again, African-Americans are being defined by others. African-Americans' imageries are developed by the hegemonic strata within the television industry (Dates, 1990). This television hegemonic strata consist of network executives, parent entities of the television networks, sponsors, writers, and producers. They are responsible for the formulation of television African-American imageries. Moreover, I have been privy to African-American producers, writers, and directors being encouraged by the television hegemonic strata to develop and film stereotypical African-American imageries.

According to Bogle (1988), African-American imageries are mostly negative. Viewing of imageries on television might be the result of imagery marketing. Television's hegemonic strata have possibly influenced the self-perceptions of African-Americans, particularly African-American young adults.

In September 1991, the National Association for the Advancement of Colored People (N.A.A.C.P.) issued a report charging the film industry with "nepotism, croneyism, and racial discrimination." Additionally, the N.A.A.C.P. stated, "Our report unhappily discloses that African-Americans are underrepresented in each and every aspect of the industry" (Robinson, 1991). The report prompted the N.A.A.C.P.'s director, Benjamin Hooks, to state in *The Times* (1991): "We may withdraw our enthusiasm for watching certain T.V. shows or movies. . . . These decision makers control the images of Blacks projected on the screen."

Increased involvement of African-Americans in television programming may result in a more accurate portrayal of African-American imageries. The African-Americans would be defining themselves for others. These imageries can reflect the diversity of attitudes, values, personalities, physical features, economics, education, politics, religion, and familial, social conditions in the African-American communities. Perhaps, the commonly portrayed imageries of African-American criminals, buffoons, illiterates, powerlessness and pathological families would be eradicated rather than inappropriately reinforced. Further, perhaps African-American viewers would feel self-empowered after viewing positive imageries of themselves.

If television's negative African-American imageries override the minds of African-Americans, then possibly those imageries can be the design for negative self-perceptions. If so, the impact of television on how African-American young adults view themselves can be ubiquitously destructive relative to self-image and self-esteem. Additionally, if African-Americans distinguish themselves as a group, there are positive implications applicable to television imageries for African-Americans that deserve attention.

The African-American young adult viewer may attribute the stereotypical characteristics of television's African-American imageries to himself or herself because many people of the same group are perceived as having the same characteristics; that is, to look, think, and behave homogeneously. Erikson (1968) stated that the self is a combination of perceptions, attitudes, and personality that are essential components for a person's identity and behavior. The controlling strata uphold their dominant positions by instituting the subservient stations of other groups (Bagley, Verma, Mallick, & Young, 1979). To institute the subservient stations or positions of African-Americans, the controlling strata must damage the self-image of African-Americans. One's positive identity and self-image are vital fundamentals for constructive self-esteem and cognitive development (Rosenbert & Simmon, 1972). Without self-esteem, what does one have? Clark and Clark (1950) stated: "It is clear that the Negro child by age five is aware of the fact that to be colored in contemporary American society is a mark of inferior status."

Again, one of the most invincible media tools is television. Mander (1978) stated:

> Seeing is believing. Like many an axiom, this one is literally true. Only since the ascendancy of the media has this been opened to question. Throughout the hundreds of thousands of generations of human existence, whatever we saw with our eyes was concrete and reliable. Experience was directly between us and the environment. Non-mediated. Non-processed. Not altered by other humans. The question of what is real and unreal is itself a new one, abstract and impossible to understand. The natural evolutionary design is for humans to see all things as real, since the things that we see have always been real.

According to the Nielsen Media Research television reports, during the months of November 1989, February 1990, May 1990, and July 1990, African-Americans viewed more television than "all other" households with few exceptions (see Appendix A for data about hours of television usage). In short, because African-American young adults view numerous hours of television, the television imageries of African-Americans may affect African-American young adults' impression of self which may impede their ability to realize their personal and academic potential in American society.

PURPOSE OF THE STUDY

The purpose of this study is to determine the possible influence of particular television imageries about African-Americans on the self-perceptions of selected young adult African-Americans, ages eighteen to twenty-five. Specifically, two research questions guide this investigation:

- What specific aspects of self are addressed by particular television imageries of African-Americans?

- What possible influences do particular television imageries have on self-perceptions of selected young adult African-Americans?

DEFINITION OF TERMS

The following definitions of five essential terms give direction to the study:

Young Adults: A young adult is a person who is between the ages of eighteen and twenty-five. A young adult's self-image may be tenuous and easily influenced because of his or her youth and immatureness relative to life's experiences.

Self-Perception: Self-perception is an awareness, cognizance, understanding, and recognition of self. Positive or negative feelings can stem from one's self-perceptions (Syngg & Coombs, 1949). Self-perceptions create significant consequences that correlate with the individual's behavior and enables a human to perceive and control his or her surroundings (Bagley, Verma, Mallick, & Young, 1979).

Television Imagery: Television programs are varied; they incorporate news coverages, commercials, comedies, dramas, music videos, and soap operas. Television imageries may embody misperceptions of people that generate prejudice, homogeneous groups and, consequently, a sustainment of America's controlling strata. Television imagery is perpetuated through episodic television programs.

Negative Imagery: Negative imagery is stereotypical imagery of a group of people which may induce a loss of self-esteem and a feeling of inferiority. Negative imagery propagandizes the 'differences' in groups who are outside of the controlling strata. Negative imagery may create negative perceptual stereotypical self-attributions. These self-attributions are inclusive of values, attitudes, behaviors, and standards (Van Dijk, 1987).

Television Hegemonic Strata: The television hegemonic strata are comprised of the Federal Communications Commission, the U. S. Senate communications committees, the parent entities that own the television networks and cable systems, network and cable executives, producers, writers, and sponsors. Those entities are responsible for instituting laws that are applicable to television programming and for dominating and fabricating television imageries.

SIGNIFICANCE OF THE STUDY

This study is important because of the following four reasons. First, learning is connected to perception. Also, there may be an equivalence between young adult African-Americans' perceptions and their realities. What humans see, what they interpret, and what they sense become the largest sensory, cognitive body of information humans deal with. The cognitive process is imbedded in how humans see it, how humans imitate it; if one sees it, one's perceptions of it may be one's reality.

One can assume that positive or negative feelings stem from one's self-perceptions (Syngg & Coombs, 1949). The self is the basis for a perception of others. The self's perceptions create significant consequences that correlate with the individual's behavior (Bagley, Verma, Mallick, & Young, 1979). Perceptions are cognitive responses to bodies of information and attitudes that are formed based on the perceptions of an object (Cacioppo, Harkins, & Petty, 1981). Finally, there are perceptions that create "out-group" discriminations and stereotypes. "Out-groups" are perceived to have "differences" that are saliently unlike the characteristics of the "in-group" (Howard & Rothbart, 1980). These "differences" relate to race, sex, skin color, hair, economic status, etc.

Second, television is a multi-dimensional auditory and visual tool that reaches multi-millions of people at any given time (Lee & Solomon, 1990). Television may be used as a tool for negative imagery marketing. If so, this means that the television hegemonic strata may be purposely constructing realities and cultivating negative self-images and perceptions of African-Americans. Hawkins and Pingree (1980) noted: "If cultivation results from learning specific symbolic messages heavily repeated in programming, then those content types where the messages are clearest and most common should be the best predictors of television bias." Research shows that television imageries of African-Americans are repetitive and clearly commonly stereotypically negative (Sutton, 1989). Additionally, the imageries are controlled and constructed by television's hegemonic strata (Dates, 1990). The present study is significant because it will contribute to greater understanding of how television imageries may have an impact on perceptions of young African-American adults.

Third, what a person "finally believes and perceives is the important thing" (Allport, 1954). The more often a person sees a portrayal, the more the person may believe the portrayal. Frequent stereotypical depictions are cultural dissonants that may create cognitive dissonances amongst African-Americans. If so, these cognitive dissonances may be equated with negative African-American television imageries. Because intergroup perceptions are referenced to similarity of self (Wilder, 1981), what African-American young adults believe, relative to seeing African-American television imageries, may have implications for self-esteem. This is another reason the present study is important.

Fourth, educators can train and educate African-American students to counter predominantly negative African-American imageries. Educators have a *responsibility* to provide quality education on equal terms for African-Americans. This equality in education will empower African-Americans to counter predominantly negative African-American television imageries. Educators have a responsibility to be honest with themselves about *their* perceptions and whether they are conveying negative perceptions and beliefs to their students. The present study is significant because it will help educators think even more carefully about their responsibilities to *all* children and young people.

As a result of this study, I hope to gain information on how education can aid in the empowerment of African-American young adults. If there are cognitive dissonances amongst African-American young adults that relate to negative television images, education may empower African-American young adults to self-define their perceptions. Ultimately, this self-empowerment should foster self-esteem for those who have for too long viewed themselves as defined by others.

LIMITATIONS OF THE STUDY

This study does not address all variables that impact on young adult African-Americans. Rather, it considers one major source of influence, which is television. Although television is an important and common source in our culture, this study does not consider all television imageries that may influence self-perceptions of African-Americans. Furthermore, the present study does not consider the television imageries that are exclusive of African-Americans. Finally, the film episodes used for the present study are extracted from one comedic television program. Inferences from the results of this research may be used to design further research. However, no generalizations should be made from this study about all African-American young adults. The generalizations should not go beyond the individuals participating in the present research.

ORGANIZATION OF THE STUDY

The book consists of five chapters. Chapter I includes the statement of the problem, purpose of the study, definition of terms, significance of the study, and limitations of the study.

Chapter II provides the conceptual base for the research. It consists of a review of literature that centers on two parts. First, the influence of perception on human behavior is considered. Second, the possible impact of television images on how individuals view themselves is reviewed.

Chapter III discusses the design of the study. The procedures for instrumentation and data collection as they relate to two specific research questions are included.

Chapter IV centers on analysis of the data and interpretation of the findings as they relate to the two major research questions that guide the investigation.

Chapter V includes a summary of the study, suggestions for further research, and recommendations for action to improve the educational intentions of television programs about African-Americans.

II

REVIEW OF THE LITERATURE

The review of literature constitutes a conceptual base for this study. Specifically, the review of related research consists of two parts. First, I considered the influence of perception on human behavior. This part of the review establishes why it is crucial to consider perceptions of individuals as a powerful force for determining how one thinks, feels, or acts. Second, I reviewed the impact of television images on how individuals view themselves. This part of the review sets forth the possibility that young adult African-Americans' views of themselves may result, in part, from African-American images they see on television (see the Bibliography, which is organized according to the two parts of the review of literature and references from other chapters).

INFLUENCE OF PERCEPTION ON HUMAN BEHAVIOR

Perception is the act of taking possession; obtaining, receiving, perceiving a mental image; awareness of the elements of environment through physical sensation; reaction to sensory color stimulus; physical sensation as interpreted in the light of experience; the integration of sensory impressions of events in the external world by a conscious organism, especially as a function of non-conscious experience derived from past experience and serving as a basis for or as verified by further meaningful motivated action. (Webster's Third New International Dictionary, 1976)

As referenced in Chapter I, what humans see, what they interpret, and what they sense becomes blended with one cognitive act (Allport, 1954). Perceptions are structured by the categories humans use to make sense of the world, which are characterized as cognitive functioning; that is, humans' perceptions of what they see may be their reality.

According to Fishbein and Ajzen (1981), cognitive functioning is divided into three categories: affect, cognition, and conation. Affect is *having* positive or negative feelings; cognition *associates* positive or negative feelings; and conation is *behaving* positively or negatively. One might like or dislike a rose; one might *feel* loving when one sees a rose; one might *be* loving when one sees a rose. Summarily, Fishbein and Ajzen theorized that an individual's behavior is "determined by the individual's attitude toward performing the behavior."

Perception is interconnected with attitude, self-esteem, prejudice, behavior, and values. The perceiver's attitude defines what someone is and what someone is not (Sherif & Sherif, 1967). Perceptions, the reality, are in "the eyes and mind of the beholder" (Snyder, Tanke, & Berscheid, 1977).

> *Individuals may have different styles of interaction for those whom they perceive to be physically attractive and for those whom they consider unattractive. Considerable evidence suggests that attractive persons are assumed to possess more socially desirable personality traits and are expected to lead better lives than their unattractive counterparts. Attractive persons are perceived to have virtually every character trait that is socially desirable to the perceiver. Physically attractive people, for example, were perceived to be more sexually warm and responsive, sensitive, kind, interesting, strong, poised, modest, sociable, and outgoing than persons of lesser physical attractiveness. (Berscheid & Walster, 1974)*

As stated in Chapter I, intergroup perception is referenced to similarity of self and the consequent; the attitude is referenced to one's group and an outside group (Wilder, 1981). One's group is "we" and out-groups are "they." (Note: I believe that humans have descriptive perceptions of what are in-groups and out-groups; therefore, there are *perceived* in-groups and *perceived* out-groups. However, to eliminate redundancy pertinent to the word perceived, I will use the words "in-group" and "out-group" throughout this chapter.)

There are perception components that create out-group discriminations, stereotypes, and reinforce intergroup superior attitudes (Taylor, Fiske, Etcoff, & Ruderman, 1978). Because of group solidarity, in-groups contrast the similarities within their groups to the dissimilarities of the out-groups (Tajfel & Wilkes, 1963). Again, these dissimilarities relate to race, sex, skin color, hair, economic status, etc. Likewise, Taylor (1981) says:

1. *People use physical and social discriminators, such as race and sex, as a way of categorizing information about them.*

2. *As a result of this categorization process, within group differences become minimized and between group differences become exaggerated (e.g., Blacks are seen as similar to each other and different from Whites).*

3. *Categorization results from a learning process and as one becomes more familiar with a given social group, categories of sub-types will develop. This process will, in turn, lead to a more highly differentiated set of stereotypes for that social group. These stereotypes will reflect, in part, the discriminating cue (i.e., kernel of truth) that is used as the basis of sub-categorization.*

Granberg's (1984) balance theory emphasizes that in-groups attribute similar attitudes and beliefs to their groups and "exaggerate the differences between their attitudes and the predominant view in an out-group." This convinces oneself that one's group is superior to another. On the other hand, Granberg's functional theory "holds that people develop, retain, and alter attitudes for value-expressive, ego-defensive knowledge, and social-adjustment purposes." In other words, the controlling group says that "others" like things the way they are. He goes on to state an example of his functional theory:

> It is only a small step to suppose that the impression people form of where others stand on a given issue can also serve a social adjustment function. Denying that Blacks in South Africa prefer a one-person, one vote situation may serve the short-term political purposes of a member of the dominant group. It was often observed that many southern Whites in the United States in the 1950s claimed that the Blacks in their area liked things the way they were. (Similar claims were made about the attitudes of slaves in an earlier era.) . . . Assimilating the views of an out-group on the matter of segregation-desegregation may have the adjustment functioning of rationalizing or buttressing one's preference in regard to changing or maintaining the status quo.

Again, in relationship to perception and cognitive functioning, humans categorize objects to simplify their environments. These categorizations affect humans' attitudes and behavior toward the objects (Wilder, 1981). To achieve attitudinal changes, the self-perception must be changed. Despite the difficulties, this might be accomplished by "a reorientation and change in roles, behaviors, values, and attitudes" (Bagley, Verma, Mallick, & Young, 1979). When humans categorize to make sense of their environment, they are forming or defining their perceptions or realities (Kelly, 1955). But some categorizations of realities or perceptions might be concocted to sustain the in-group's or controlling strata's hold on power. Although in-groups perceive out-groups to be 'different,' the in-groups perceive themselves, as members, to be heterogenous and the out-groups' members to be homogeneous. That is, in-group members can have diversified personalities, life's experiences, etc. Out-group members are given negative attributions by the in-group and the perceived diversification of out-groups has been diminished (Tajfel, 1981). Examples of negative attributions are: lazy, insignificant, criminal, unclean, ignorant, etc. Moreover, it may be possible that people perceive *themselves* to be out-group members, thereby attributing negative attributions to themselves.

Hamilton and Rose (1980) said:

> *Stereotypic judgements can be viewed as expressing the perceiver's belief regarding a correlational relationship between two variables, one having to do with group membership and the other being a psychological attribute. Thus, for example, the statement 'Blacks are lazy' does not mean that 'Blacks, just like everyone else, are lazy'; rather, it states a relationship between blackness and laziness that by implication includes the assertion that non-blackness is associated with lesser degrees of laziness. . . . Given some stereotypic expectation about a group, the processing of information about members of that group would be biased. . . . The result for the perceiver would be a subjective confirmation of his or her stereotypic expectation in which blackness would be seen as related to laziness, even though no such relationship existed in the information to which the person would maintain the perceiver's perception of the 'validity' of the stereotypic belief and thereby make it resistant to change.*

Self-image and self-esteem relate to perceptions of one's group (Norton, 1983). Beliefs relating to out-groups that are inclusive of stereotypical differences, and how stereotypes affect someone's perceptions of an individual representative of another group, have been researched by Duncan (1976). Hamilton (1979) discussed the biased encoding of information relating to groups when he noted that most out-group members are easily identifiable by salient characteristics, such as hair, skin color, facial features, etc. For instance, Poussaint (1974) noted:

> *Black children, like all children, come into the world victims of factors over which they have no control. In the looking glass of White society, the*

supposedly undesirable physical image of 'tar baby' . . . is contrasted unfavorably with the valued model of 'Snow White' . . . white skin, straight hair, and aquiline features.

Hamilton (1981) stated that humans tend to interpret information based on their preconceptions of groups. Predictably, many of these preconceptions are forms of prejudice. Prejudice is "a culturally predetermined, biased attitude toward or conception of a person or group" (Young & Mack, 1962). Allport (1954) defined prejudice as "a hostile attitude toward a person who belongs to a group, simply because he belongs to that group, and is therefore presumed to have the objectionable qualities ascribed to the group." Furthermore, people may or may not think well of someone without a significant reason. For example, no one knows *all* Catholics, *all* Chinese, *all* African-Americans, *all* elderly people, etc.

As well, Allport (1954) says:

Negative attitude tends to express itself in action. Certain degrees of negative action are:

1. *Antilocution: Most people who have prejudices talk about them. With like-minded friends, occasionally with strangers, they may express their antagonism freely.*

2. *Avoidance: If the prejudice is more intense, it leads the individual to avoid members of the disliked group.*

3. *Discrimination: Here the prejudiced person makes detrimental distinctions of an active sort. He undertakes to exclude all members of the group in question from certain types of employment, from residential housing, political rights, educational or recreational opportunities, churches, hospitals, or from some other social privileges.*

> 4. *Physical Attack: Under conditions of heightened emotion, prejudice may lead to acts of violence or semi-violence.*
>
> 5. *Extermination: Lynchings, pogroms, and massacres mark the ultimate degree of violent expression of prejudice.*

People have a tendency to see and perceive people with a racial slant. These attitudinal perceptions can be reinforced through communications (Van Dijk, 1987). Van Dijk researched the efficacy of communications relating to prejudice to determine how in-groups "engage in conversations about ethnic minority groups; and how the in-groups report to each other." Fishbein and Ajzen (1981) said, "Information is the essence of the persuasion process. Receivers are exposed to a persuasive communication in the hope that they will be influenced by the information it contains. The effectiveness of the message depends in large measure on the nature of this information."

This communication upholds the principles of heterogeneity and similarities of the in-groups and the "differences" and homogeneity of the out-groups. Furthermore, Van Dijk (1987) explained that prejudice is "a group attitude" that is a common property of the in-group; the out-groups are believed to be "different on any social dimension"; the "perceived ethnic differences of the out-group" are labelled "negatively" compared to the "values, interests, and norms of the in-group"; the "ethnic attitude is used in social context as the cognitive program for intergroup preception and interaction that is structurally favorable for the in-group. In this respect, ethnic prejudice is the cognitive foundation of racism." L. Barry proclaimed that "any perceivable difference is an opportunity for hierarchy, and human beings grab at the opportunity" (Rothstein, 1991).

Attitudes and prejudiced behaviors are interrelated; the attitude is the antecedent to the behavior. Attitudes are the bases for the categorizations of groups. Ehrlich (1973) found that persons who committed prejudiced aggression liked to find scapegoat groups that are vulnerable to attack. On the other hand, Ehrlich found that the in-groups often blame the out-groups for prejudiced aggression. There are numerous media reports, with pictures of the out-group members, who are cited for crimes that sustain the negative perceptions, attitudes, and beliefs relating to these biased reports. Moreover, the in-group rationalizes why it has to jail the out-group members by saying that it must protect the in-group from potential out-group aggression. Mostly, the in-group members are perceived to be the likely victims of the out-groups.

Because there is so much rejection of out-groups that stems from prejudice, there is the issue of self-esteem for out-group members. There appears to be an organized, consistent attempt to diminish the self-esteem of out-groups. Out-groups are usually defined by negative characterizations: African-Americans are criminals; Native-Americans are savages; Mexicans are lazy; Chinese people are sly. *Webster's Dictionary* (1976) defines red as an American Indian; redskin; (risking himself on a wearied horse in a country alive with Indians); subversive, revolutionary; communist. Yellow is defined as yellowed, shallow; having a yellow or mulatto complexion or skin; jaundiced, jealous; mean, dishonorable. As stated in Chapter I, black is defined as "soiled with dirt, dirty; outrageously wicked; deserving unmitigated condemnation; expressing or indicating disgrace, dishonor, discredited; or guilt, and dark in comparison to the average complexion of a group." Conversely, white is described as a color like that of new snow or clean milk; of the color white (well bleached linen is perfectly white); being of White ancestry either wholly unmixed with Negro blood or having a mixture of Negro blood less than specified in various statues of some states in the United States; straightforward and kindly; square dealing.

These statements of meaning are permeated throughout society. What schools, libraries, and homes do not have dictionaries? Perhaps these definitions are intended to counter and ruin the development of self-esteem of out-group members.

Banks (1972) declared "Black children derive their conceptions of themselves largely from White society and their institutions" (see Figure 1). Furthermore, Dennis (1981) stated:
According to Clark (1955, pp. 25-26), children's attitudes toward Blacks are determined chiefly 'not by contact with Negroes but by contacts with prevailing attitudes toward Negroes.' Clark concludes that it is the idea of Blacks rather than any particular characteristics of Blacks that evokes hostility toward them.
Allport (1954) believed that "the stereotype plays a prominent part in sharpening the perceptions prior to actions" (see Figure 2). The confirmation of stereotypes amplifies a human's belief in the stereotype (Gurwitz & Dodge, 1977). Conversely, Gurwitz and Dodge (1977) set forth that "it may be that when one person's behaviors are completely inconsistent with the stereotype, the disconfirming evidence becomes too salient to be discounted, resulting in a decreased use of the stereotype in making inferences about other group members."
Moreover, Weber and Crocker (1983) state:
Disconfirming information exhibited by unrepresentative members is used to create new subtypes. . . . Group members who dramatically disconfirm the stereotype will potentially change stereotypes more because they are clearly disconfirming. . . . When information about many members was given (large sample condition), disconfirming evidence changed stereotypes more when it was dispersed than when it was concentrated.
There is a differentiation between an attitude and a value. According to Rokeach (1973), an attitude "refers to an organization of several beliefs" and a value "refers to a single belief." Woodruff (1942) stated that "attitudes are functions of values." Humans have values; humans sense, perceive, experience, confirm, and react to their values. Values and needs are analogous with feelings of oughtness; "a wish to do it" (Rokeach, 1973). Humans utilize values for self-realization.
Values set the standards for ourselves (the self) to others

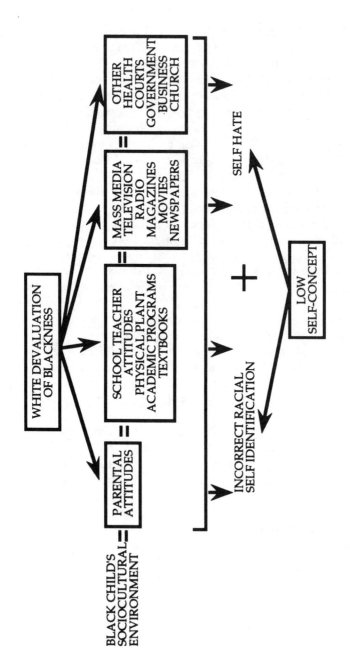

Figure 1. Social determinants of the Black child's self-concept (Banks, 1972).

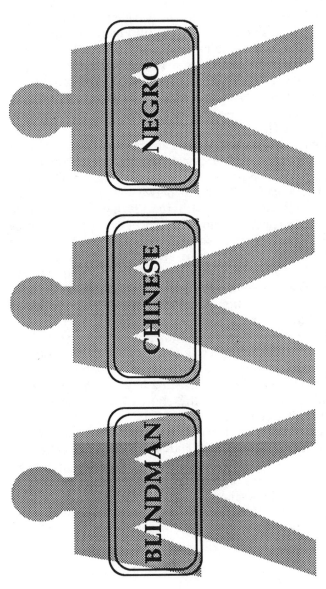

Figure 2. The effect of linguistic symbols upon perception and thinking about individuals (Allport, 1954).

(Goffman, 1959) and to pronounce an opinion about others, thereby influencing our beliefs about race. For example, Moynihan (1966, 1967), in his Moynihan Report, claimed that African-Americans' families are malfunctioning, inducing social ills, such as "unemployment, personality ills, poverty, etc." Additionally, Moynihan stated that African-Americans are a subculture that self-perpetuates a subculture of poverty, and the African-American people have "distinct attributes" of that subculture that are socialized through each generation of mercurial families.

Rokeach (1973) tested Moynihan's report. Rokeach used equivalent groups of African-Americans and White-Americans that transcended all economical and educational classifications to determine what "differences" between the groups might materialize. He found that differences that evolved were relevant to "socioeconomic differences rather than race differences." Moreover, Rokeach found that the only value that was ostentatiously different between African-Americans and White-Americans was equality (see Table 1). He established that if the "socioeconomic status is held constant, most of the value differences become minimal, with the exception of the differences concerning equality."

Values are interconnected with perceptions; values are believed to be the interpretations of peoples' perceptions, attitudes, and behaviors. Rogers (1989) established that as an infant matures, he or she is persuaded by others to internalize others' values; e.g., parents, the church, radio, the printed word, or any visual forms of media.

In conclusion, again, humans' perceptions are intertwined with attitudes, self-esteem, prejudice, behavior, and values. Furthermore, perceptions, attitudes, self-esteem, prejudice, behavior, and values appear to be learned from others' influences or predominance. Therewith, the others' influences may sway how one thinks, feels, and/or acts. Can some of the influences be television imageries?

Table 1

Terminal Value Composite Rank Orders for White and Black
Americans Matched for Income and Education (N=396)

Value	White (N=198)	Black (N=198)
A Comfortable Life	7	5
An Exciting Life	18	18
A Sense of Accomplishment	11	11
A World of Beauty	15	16
A World of Peace	1	1
Equality	12	2
Family Security	2	4
Freedom	3	3
Happiness	4	6
Inner Harmony	13	12
Mature Love	14	14
National Security	9	13
Pleasure	17	17
Salvation	5	9
Self-Respect	6	7
Social Recognition	16	15
True Friendship	8	10
Wisdom	10	8

From *The Nature of Human Values* by M. Rokeach, 1973
(New York: Free Press).

Note: Rokeach described terminal values as being
"self-centered or society-centered, intrapersonal or
interpersonal in focus." The figures shown are the
composite rank orders.

THE IMPACT OF TELEVISION IMAGES ON
HOW INDIVIDUALS VIEW THEMSELVES

In the early part of the twentieth century, movie studios and/or producers, directors, and writers developed imageries of African-Americans. What Hollywood asked for is what was designed for the public's entertainment.

Later, many of these movies were oftentimes aired on television.

Sinclair (1991) wrote:

> *Hollywood was creating a lot of excitement in America. It was also an important vehicle for assorted messages. Hollywood producers learned early that people paid to see what they wanted to see, even if it was a fantasy. So loving darkies, sambos, hefty Black maids who smiled and cooked all day, lazy Blacks who were lucky to live on a plantation taking advantage of a doting benign master, if these images were no longer to be had in real life, they were to be had on the screen. And indeed were used to reinforce lost dominance.*

Because these imageries were/are established in the minds of American viewers, these imageries might be perceived as *real* representations of African-Americans. Are African-Americans' views of themselves reflective of these imageries (see Figures 3, 4, 5, 6, and 7)?

To understand the possible impact of television imageries on humans' self-perceptions, I will review Bogle's (1989) literature on the characters who were portrayed as the Toms, coons, mulattoes, mammies, and bucks in American movies in the beginning of the twentieth century.

I abbreviated definitions and quotations from Bogle's work relative to the aforementioned characters, some of the films depicting each character and studios and/or the producers that were responsible for the development of the characters, follows. (Note: Bogle used the words *colored, Negro,* and *Black* as they were used *in their proper historical context.*)

• **The Tom.** The Tom is a socially acceptable *Good Negro* character. Toms are chased, harassed, hounded, flogged,

See Author's Note

Figure 3. Scene depicting the tar and feathering of an African-American child and his dog.

See Author's Note

Figure 4. Scene from *Little Daddy*.

See Author's Note

Figure 5. Scene from *Gone With The Wind*, a David O. Selznick Technicolor Production released by Metro-Goldwyn-Mayer in 1939.

See Author's Note

Figure 6. Scene from *The Country Chairman*, a Fox Film
Production.

See Author's Note

Figure 7. Scene from *The Stu Erwin Show*.

insulted, never turned against their White massas, and remained submissive, generous, and kind. Thus, they endear themselves to White audiences.

In 1927, Universal Pictures filmed "Uncle Tom's Cabin", a story about a *good Christian slave*. Universal Pictures promoted its *good colored star* with this release:

> *James B. Lowe has made history. A history that reflects only credit to the Negro race not only because he has given the 'Uncle Tom' character a new slant, but because of his exemplary conduct with the Universal Company. They look upon Lowe at the Universal Studio as a living Black god. . . . Of the directors, critics, artists, and actors who have seen James Lowe work at the Studio, there are none who will not say he is the most suited of all men for the part of 'Tom'. Those who are religious say that a heavenly power brought him to Universal and all predict a most marvelous future and worldwide reputation for James B. Lowe. (Bogle, 1989, p. 6)*

• **The Coon.** The Coon is a *Black buffoon* who lacks the single-mindedness of the Tom. There are three types of Coons: the pickaninny, the pure Coon, and the Uncle Remus.

The "pickaninny" is a harmless Negro child whose eyes pop and whose hair stands on end with the least excitement.

In 1922, Hal Roach produced a comedy series of short films, titled "Our Gang". "Our Gang" featured a pickaninny character named Farina. Farina had tightly twisted pigtails that stood up when he was frightened, and old patched gingham clothes. The "Our Gang" series was one of Roach's successful creations.

Later, the "pure Coon" was developed. This character is unreliable, crazy, lazy, a subhuman creature who does nothing but eat watermelons, steals chickens, and butchers the English language. The pure Coon was blatantly the most degrading of Black stereotypes.

In the 1930s, the pure Coon character was fabricated by Fox Pictures. Stepin Fetchit, the character actor, became the most successful Black actor working in Hollywood in the 1930s. He was hired to popularize the pure Coon character.

In the 1930s, Fetchit teamed in four films with Will Rogers, a famous White actor. Fetchit was cast as an inarticulate, backward handyman for Will Rogers. Throughout these films, the Stepin Fetchit cowered, shuffled, and/or rendered himself almost unintelligible. Usually, he was demeaned and racially degraded. For example, in "David Harum," he is traded to Will Rogers along with a horse.

"Uncle Remus" is harmless, congenial, quaint, and naive. He is satisfied with the system and his place in it.

In 1936, Warner Brothers filmed "The Green Pastures", which turned out to be one of the most successful movies about Negroes of all time. "The Green Pastures" was inclusive of the Toms, Coons, Uncle Remus, and mammy characters. This movie utilized so-called Negro colloquialisms. "Beine de Lawd ain't no bed of roses," moans the heavenly host. "Now you heared me. You want me to fly up there and slap you down?" Ultimately, "The Green Pastures" became a perpetual Negro holiday, one everlasting weekend fish fry.

• **The Mulatto.** The mulatto is likable and sympathetic only because she is half White. The audience is led to believe that the mulatto's life could have been productive and happy if she were not a victim of a divided racial inheritance.

In 1949, Twentieth Century Fox Studio produced "Pinky", a story about the tragic mulatto. Pinky, who had been passing for White in the North, had decided to sacrifice personal happiness by remaining with "her people" in the South.

• **The Mammy.** The mammy closely relates to the comic Coons; however, the mammy is distinguished by her sex and her fierce independence. She is usually big, fat, and cantankerous.

Mammy's offshoot is the Aunt Jemima. Conversely, Aunt Jemimas are sweet, good-tempered, and blessed with religion.

In 1939, David O. Selznick produced "Gone With The Wind," featuring a faithful, enslaved mammy as one of the primary movie characters. True to the studio's fabricated mammy characterizations, Mammy (this film character's name) is big, fat, and fiercely independent. She berates anyone who goes against *her* conception of right and wrong. As all movie mammies, Mammy devoted her life to the caring of her slave owners.

- **The Buck.** The buck was often represented as the brutal Black buck. The Black bucks are always big, bad, oversexed, savage, violent, and frenzied, as they lust for White flesh. The infamous film "The Birth of a Nation" was written, produced, and directed by D. W. Griffith in 1915. Griffith's buck characters were the archetypical figures; Griffith played on the myth of the Negro's high-powered sexuality.

In articulating his thesis, Griffith seemed to be saying that things were in order only when Whites were in control and when the American Negro was kept in his place. This film became one of the highest grossing movies of all time.

Gerbner and Gross (1976) suggest a relationship between television viewing and television biased constructions of reality. Hawkins and Pingree (1980) noted, "If cultivation results from learning specific symbolic messages heavily repeated in programming, then those content types where the messages are clearest and most common should be the best predictors of television bias."

Perceived negative stereotypical attributions are bolstered by "persuasive communication" that are intended to have a bearing on the beliefs of the receivers of those messages (Fishbein & Ajzen, 1981). Processing the information that is formulated from the persuasive communication "is classifying, contrasting, and judging oneself and others" (Nisbett & Ross, 1980).

Moreover, Postman (1982) said that "people watch television, not read it. It is the picture that dominates the viewers' consciousness. . . . Watching television requires instantaneous pattern-recognition, not delayed analytic decoding. It requires perception, not conception."

Social scientists have reported diversified hypotheses about television's effects on people. Klapper (1954) was of the opinion that television exposure negatively affects children's perceptions; that television made children apathetic who sat and viewed television for lengthy time periods. Additionally,

Klapper believed that if children viewed violent shows, these children would behave violently.

Comstock, Chaffee, Katzman, McCombs, and Roberts (1978) found that "new research is finding that under some circumstances, television may influence behavior and attitudes other than those related to aggressiveness." They went on to say:

> *We posit that television can affect the salience of an act in two ways: by demonstrating the act, and by attaching negative or positive values to the act. . . . It seems intuitively obvious that the more often, and the more vividly, a given act is portrayed for a person, the more salient it will become to him.*

As mentioned in Chapter I, the more often a person sees a portrayal, the more the person may believe the portrayal. Kunjufu (1984) says that humans are influenced by television images of "places and times and people and stories with which we've never had contact." Furthermore, Kunjufu queries: "Once television provides an image of places and times, what happens to your own image? Does it give way to the T.V. image or do you retain it?"

Some social scientists have questioned whether television is responsible for people perceiving themselves as being violent. Radecki (1991) states in *U.S.A. Today*:

> *At this year's meeting of the American Psychiatric Association, Dr. Brandon Centenvall gave strong evidence that T.V. and film violence is the cause of fully 50% of the crime and violence in our society and two other countries studied. He estimates there would be 10,000 fewer murders, 70,000 fewer rapes, one million fewer motor vehicle thefts, 2.5 million fewer burglaries, and 10 million fewer larcenies here each year if not for violent T.V. and film entertainment. (p. 10)*

Furthermore, McLeod, Atkins, and Chaffee (1972) said that adolescents who felt very aggressive and/or violent after viewing television were relating to their perceived realities based on television content. In 1973, Surgeon General Steinfeld expressed concern about the relationship between "televised violence and anti-social behavior." Osborn and Endsley (1971) said that television content created a perceived reality of fear. On the other hand, Greenfield and Beagles-Roos (1988) researched the impact of television versus radio on children. They stated: "From a historical point of view, the growing importance of television means that children socialized by this medium may have more information but be less imaginative, less verbally precise, and less mentally active than an earlier generation for whom radio was a major medium of socialization."

Tan and Tan (1979) have researched television viewing and self-esteem in African-American adults. They found that African-American adults' self-esteem was negatively affected by many hours of television viewing. Barnes (1980) believed that television images of African-Americans are negative; therefore, African-American children viewers might internalize the messages that they are unimportant people in African society. Warren (1988) said, "The image, that is, the impression, idea, and concept, of Black people in the United States is heavily influenced by the projections we see on film and on television. To what extent people are influenced by images is still being researched, but that images do have an effect is without doubt."

The following images, excerpted out of Warren's (1988) references from Reddick (1975), are, according to Warren, those which appear in all media. According to Reddick, they are:

- Savage African
- Happy slave
- Devoted servant
- Corrupt politician
- Irresponsible citizen
- Petty thief
- Social delinquent
- Vicious criminal
- Sexual superman
- Unhappy non-White
- Natural-born cook
- Perfect entertainer

- Superstitious churchgoer
- Chicken and watermelon eater
- Razor and knife "toter"
- Uninhibited expressionist
- Mentally inferior
- Natural-born musician

Warren goes on to say: "All of the stereotypes found in literature, on the stage, and on radio are captured and reinforced by the camera's eye."

I will now list some of the television shows, featuring African-American characterizations, that have been "reinforced by the camera's eye." The reader may contrast these characterizations with Reddick's (1975) list of aforementioned imageries. These television shows are concomitant with the identities of the networks and the air dates. The following facts are extractions from Bogle (1988):

- "Amen", N.B.C. (Premiered September 1, 1986): This series featured a church deacon, who verbally barks and bites at just about anybody; he has a great deal of old-style hootin' and hollerin'.
- "Amos 'n' Andy", C.B.S. (June, 1951 to June, 1953): This series encompassed all stereotypes of African-Americans; such as asexual Black women and inferior, lazy, dumb, dishonest, and loud characters.
- "Benson", A.B.C. (September 13, 1979 to August 30, 1986): Initially, Benson was a happy, contented servant who found satisfaction in his work while developing affection for the White folks who employed him.
- "Beulah", A.B.C. (October 3, 1950 to September 22, 1953): Beulah was a friendly Black maid, who was so caught up in her White employers' lives, that she had very little life of her own.
- "Gimme a Break", N.B.C. (Premiered October 29, 1981): This series featured a Black housekeeper working for a White family. This housekeeper was sassy and gutsy.
- "Good Times", C.B.S. (February 8, 1974 to August 1, 1979): This series was the 1970s first Black family sitcom whose famous character, J.J., was barely literate. This character prompted Esther Rolle, one of

this series' actresses, to say in *Ebony*, "I resent the imagery that says to Black kids that you can make it by standing on the corner saying 'Dyn-O-Mite'! He's eighteen and he doesn't work. He can't read or write. He doesn't think. The show didn't start out to be that. Little by little . . . they have made J.J. more stupid and enlarged the role. Negative images have been quietly slipped in on us through the character of the oldest child."

- "That's My Mama", A.B.C. (September 4, 1974 to December 24, 1975): This series featured many stereotypical characters; mainly an all-sacrificing, large, warm-hearted mammy and a lively, but emasculated, Black female-dominated home that television always seems comfortable with.

- "Diff'rent Strokes", N.B.C.; later moved to A.B.C. (November 3, 1978 to August 30, 1986): This series focused on African-American male children who are raised by a White man. These children do not have any Black relatives or Black friends; there is not a Black community to speak of in this series.

- "Sanford and Son", N.B.C. (January 14, 1972 to September 2, 1977): This series featured two Black men who lived in a junkyard. These characters were harmless and naive.

Again, are African-Americans' views of themselves reflective of these imageries?

In closing, Sinclair (1991) made public this statement:

Films, movies, television, and indeed all media have had and continue to have a profound effect on the personality of the people who watch them. . . . Films set the pace, the tone of living in America. They told America what was beautiful and what was not, what was funny, and what was truth and what wasn't. They defined America's enemies, labeled her friends, and almost single-handedly rewrote American history to suit the fantasies of people already corrupted by racism and slavery. . . .

> *Films miseducated America, created a market with lies, then stimulated the market.*

Additionally, Dates (1990), pronounced:

> *Television of the 1990s, as a purveyor of shared cultural values, must deal with relevant issues, and present contemporary concepts and stories characteristic of America's multicultural, multiethnic society, and do so with a balance view rather than a one-sided and dominant culture-controlled one. . . . It is my opinion that the infusion of authentic, African-American controlled images into mainstream popular culture, particularly television, could help all Americans better understand themselves.*

This chapter centered on two main themes: the influence of perception on human behavior and the impact of television images on how individuals view themselves. This chapter provided a conceptual base for supporting the purpose of the study. Furthermore, it gives direction to the design of the study, because the design of the study highlights the perceptions of people.

III

DESIGN OF THE STUDY

For the design of this exploratory study, I used a qualitative methodology to answer the research questions. I consider this approach an appropriate form of inquiry because of my years of personal and business experiences relative to the infrastructure of the television medium. Additionally, I conducted interviews in the interviewees' community.

According to Patton (1991), one major theme of qualitative inquiry is personal contact and insight. Patton states the following: "The researcher has direct contact with and gets close to the people, situation, and phenomenon under study; the researcher's personal experiences and insights are an important part of the inquiry and critical to understanding the phenomenon."

The design of the present study centers on two major questions that are embraced in the purpose statement. Each question is stated and the steps for answering each question are detailed.

QUESTION 1: WHAT SPECIFIC ASPECTS OF SELF ARE ADDRESSED BY PARTICULAR TELEVISION IMAGERIES OF AFRICAN-AMERICANS?

Sequentially, to conduct this study, I took the following steps. First, I selected one comedic television program to be used in this study. A representative of this comedic television program was contacted by me to randomly select twenty sample shows, ten shows from 1990 and ten shows from 1991. The program has existed for only these two years.

Second, I wrote numbers on cards that corresponded with the twenty sample shows. Next, the 1990 and 1991 cards were placed, according to year, in two separate containers. Without looking in the containers, I pulled two numbers from each container.

Third, to determine if the four randomly selected shows were centering on African-Americans, I selected three African-American young adults to view the four sample shows. The criteria for the selection of panel members included their familiarity with this particular television program and their lack of negative or positive biases about the television program. I interviewed potential panel members to determine if they met the criteria. A judge was selected to validate my decision about the appropriateness of panel members.

One of the four randomly selected shows was not approved by the panel; therefore, I repeated the aforementioned method of random selection to replace the unapproved show.

Fourth, after the young adult African-American panelists reviewed and approved the four sample shows, they returned the shows to me.

Fifth, I selected three African-American judges: one social psychologist, one anthropologist, and one psychiatrist who specializes in counseling young adults between the ages of seventeen to thirty. Because the present study focuses on young adult African-Americans' perceptions of self, I believe that it is important to have professional insights into specific aspects of self that are addressed by particular television imageries about African-Americans.

I sent letters to request participation to each judge. The letters included a request for each judge's resume and a written response to me.

As mentioned earlier, the design of the study is arranged around two research questions that are included in the purpose statement in Chapter I. To answer Question 1, the judges were sent the four shows and a letter of instructions which included the following steps. First, the judges viewed the four shows. Each show embodied twenty to thirty minutes and approximately five episodes. Second, I asked the judges to identify and analyze the positive and/or negative imageries that they thought may influence the self-concept of African-American young adults (see Appendix B for the judges' response sheet). The judges' completed and sent their responses to me.

Sixth, to review and evaluate what commonalities prevailed in the judges' analyses, I constructed a judges' data matrix (see Table 2). This matrix enabled me to record the judges' analyses relative to positive and negative imageries that were applicable to every show and each episode. Furthermore, and finally, I constructed three subquestions to guide the analysis for Question 1. They are as follows:

- **Subquestion I:** What did the three judges determine were the positive or negative influences of the selected episodes on self?

- **Subquestion II:** What does each judge consider to be the major likely influences on self?

- **Subquestion III:** What likely influences were identified by all of the judges in the selected episodes?

I then used the data that were generated from the matrix and subquestion analyses of the three judges to answer Research Question 1.

QUESTION 2: WHAT POSSIBLE INFLUENCES DO PARTICULAR TELEVISION IMAGERIES HAVE ON SELF-PERCEPTIONS OF SELECTED YOUNG ADULT AFRICAN-AMERICANS?

Following are the steps that were taken to answer Question 2. First, I asked one member of the New York academic community and one sociologist to serve as interviewers. Respectively, the interviewers were members of Canaan Baptist Church and Shiloh Baptist Church in Harlem, New York. I wanted the interviewers to be immersed in the Harlem community to gain access to the young adult residents of Harlem. I selected Harlem because it is the largest African-American community in the United States. Therefore, Harlem provides important symbolic significance for the study.

Under my direction, the interviewers selected ten young adult African-Americans, who were likewise members of the aforementioned churches, to participate in the study. I gave a list of criteria to the interviewers that was utilized to make the final selection of the young adult African-Americans. The criteria included diverse economic and educational backgrounds, equal representations of both sexes, an ability to articulate his or her thoughts and feelings, and to be African-American young adults between the ages of eighteen and twenty-five.

After speaking to several young adult African-Americans, the interviewers made a final selection of five men and five women. Decisions were made by the interviewers to match the criteria for the purposeful sample. After the selections, the interviews were terminated.

Second, I contacted the Apollo Theatre in Harlem, New York, to request use of a room that contained a television, tape player, and a video machine. I asked to reserve this room for two weeks. The interviewers asked the selected young adult African-Americans to individually report to the Apollo Theatre at an appointed time.

Subsequently, one prospective male participant cancelled his appointment; therefore, I asked the assistant studio manager of the Apollo Theatre to select a young adult male replacement from the Apollo Theatre's list of employees. The assistant studio manager utilized the identical list of criteria that was distributed to the preexistent interviewers. After the selection, I had five men and five women who participated in the study.

I had a private three-hour session with each individual. I audiotaped each participant's session and I had an assistant who operated all machinery. This freed me to be fully attentive to interviewing the participants. I asked each participant to fill out a participant consent form.

Third, each participant viewed the identical shows that were given to the judges. The shows were sequential, e.g., Show I, Show II, Show III, Show IV. Because each show contained approximately five episodes, I stopped the show after each episode to orally question the participants about their perceptions of the episode. Before the questions were asked, I gave the participant a period of reflection. Presumably, this established the mind-set for the participant, to report possible influences of the images in the episode on their self-perceptions.

I asked the same questions after each episode of each show: As an African-American, what does this episode make you think about yourself? As an African-American, how does this episode make you feel about yourself? If time permitted, I added three more questions: Would you feel differently about yourself and/or this episode if you viewed this episode with a White-American audience versus an African-American audience? What would you think about yourself and/or this episode if you knew that the world's populace were viewing it? What do you think other ethnic people would learn from this episode? After the participants completed the interview session, I gave each participant a free ticket to attend a show at the Apollo Theatre to show appreciation for their time and effort.

Fourth, after completing the private sessions with all participants, I had the audiotapes transcribed. Data about perceptions resulting from the shows were organized by constructing a Researcher's Data Matrix (see Table 3) that was similar to the Judges' Data Matrix (see Table 2). Specifically, I read the transcripts of the sessions and marked on the matrix the number of positive and negative responses to the imageries that were viewed by each young adult African-American. Furthermore, I established a profile from a personal history form (see Appendix C for "Personal History Form" and "Profiles of Interviewees").

Finally, I composed three subquestions that guided the analysis of Question 2. They are as follows:

- **Subquestion I:** Did the interviewees perceive the episodes to be positive or negative relative to their self-perceptions of African-Americans?

- **Subquestion II:** What were the positive and negative influences of the episodes as reported by the interviewees?

- **Subquestion III:** What changes in perceptions took place when the interviewees considered what other ethnic audiences may think about African-Americans as a result of the episodes' images?

I then used the data that were generated from the matrix and subquestion analyses of the ten young adult African-American participants to answer Research Question 2.

IV

PRESENTATION AND ANALYSIS OF THE DATA

This chapter embodies data relative to two research questions presented in Chapters I and III. The research questions are:

- **Question 1:** What specific aspects of self are addressed by particular television imageries of African-Americans?

- **Question 2:** What possible influences do particular television imageries have on self-perceptions of selected young adult African-Americans?

The sources of information for the analyses of these questions were three judges and ten interviewees. The judges and interviewees were discussed in Chapter III. The three judges (Dr. Kenneth B. Clark, Dr. Johnnetta B. Cole, and Dr. Alvin F. Poussaint) provided thought-provoking analyses relative to the first question. The ten interviewees (Leroy, Keri, John, Ahmed, Elizabeth, Barbara, Lisa, Thelma, David, and Gordon) were young adult African-Americans between the ages of eighteen and twenty-five. They were punctual, cooperative, and enlightening (see Appendix C for "Profiles of Interviewees").

The judges and the interviewees supplied substantial data that, hopefully, will be used to initiate further research. Once more, the multidimensional components of this topic were restricted within the limitations of this study.

QUESTION 1: WHAT SPECIFIC ASPECTS OF SELF ARE ADDRESSED BY PARTICULAR TELEVISION IMAGERIES OF AFRICAN-AMERICANS?

To analyze the data relative to Question 1 ("What specific aspects of self are addressed by particular television imageries of African-Americans?"), I composed three subquestions. I sectioned each subquestion using the judges' data.

Subquestion I: What Did the Three Judges Determine Were the Positive or Negative Influences of the Selected Episodes on Self?

Table 2 shows the three judges' responses on the "Judges' Data Matrix".

Positive or Negative Influences Reported by Judge – Dr. Kenneth B. Clark. The first judge, Dr. Kenneth B. Clark, identified seventeen negative influences on self-concept from a total of nineteen episodes. The following statements are some of Dr. Clark's data pertinent to the "negative" influences on self-concept:

SHOW I, EPISODE 1

Negative Imageries: The caricature of Jesse Jackson as President of the United States offers the possibility of a Black being president is a comedy.

Likely Influence on Self-Concept: Young Blacks could see themselves as being funny in any serious political position; therefore, a likely influence on self-concept would be negative.

SHOW I, EPISODE 3

Negative Imageries: The character's role is potentially subhuman, if not almost animalistic.

Likely Influence on Self-Concept: There is a disturbing negative influence on self-concept in depicting Blacks as subhuman.

Table 2

Judges' Data Matrix

		Judge #1 Dr. Kenneth B. Clark		Judge #2 Dr. Johnnetta B. Cole		Judge #3 Dr. Alvin F. Poussaint	
SHOW	EPISODE	+	–	+	–	+	–
I	1		–		–		–
I	2		–		–		–
I	3		–		–		–
I	4		–		–		–
I	5		–		–		–
II	1		–		–		–
II	2		–		–	+	
II	3		–		–		–
II	4	+			–		–
II	6	+			–		–
III	1		–		–	+	
III	2		–		–		–
III	3		–		–	+	
III	4		–		–		–
III	5		–		–		–
IV	1		–		–		–
IV	2		–		–		–
IV	4		–		–	+	
IV	5		–		–		–

+ = Positive
– = Negative
+/– = Positive/Negative (Hybrid)

SHOW I, EPISODE 5

Negative Imageries: The entire episode is a negative image; it destructively humorizes drug addicts, the homeless, and the poor. Moreover, this episode disgustingly pokes fun at economic and racial tragedy.

Likely Influence on Self-Concept: There are negative images created by a Black actor; thus, making all the images acceptable parts of African-American culture.

SHOW II, EPISODE 1

Negative Imageries: A Black man is portrayed as a silly-looking clown who curses, strikes women, and has spent "eight years in prison."

Likely Influence on Self-Concept: This portrayal justifies anti-establishment, anti-social, and deviant behavior.

SHOW II, EPISODE 3

Negative Imageries: There is stereotypical joking toward home, family, poverty, and especially children ("crack addict in the making").

Likely Influence on Self-Concept: This justifies and almost glorifies negative Black stereotypes.

SHOW III, EPISODE 3

Negative Imageries: Black athletes' primary concern is learning to dance in the end zone after scoring a touchdown. Additionally, there is a portrayal of a stereotyped gay choreographer coach.

Likely Influence on Self-Concept: The Black athletes' imagery is detrimental in that it tends to negate the positive contributions of Black athletes. The choreographer's image makes fun of gays.

SHOW III, EPISODE 4

Negative Imageries: This episode ridicules Black poverty, Blacks in general; and it implies that Blacks lack talent.

Likely Influence on Self-Concept: These imageries leave nothing for Black youth to aspire to.

SHOW IV, EPISODE 5

Negative Imageries: A most complicatedly disturbing set of images: the clown is symbolically equated to the Black male ("stupid clown trick" equals stupid Black male trick); not a clown, but a faithful and humble buffoon; join the establishment and shame yourself.

Likely Influence on Self-Concept: The implications are very significant, but they would be difficult for the majority of young people to grasp; any association of a clown with a Black male could only have a negative impact.

Conversely, Dr. Clark contributed data that relate to the "positive" influences on self-concept.

SHOW II, EPISODE 4

Positive Imageries: This is a generally clever, one-man show.

Likely Influence on Self-Concept: This image could possibly have a positive self-concept influence; there isn't any stereotyped projection. There is a positive self-image without words being spoken.

SHOW II, EPISODE 6

Positive Imageries: There is a positive interaction between parents and children.

Likely Influence on Self-Concept: This episode reflects family stability almost neutralized by exaggerated head size and its symbolism.

Again, Dr. Clark found seventeen negative influences on self-concept and two positive influences on self-concept. The negative influences on self-concept were reported by this judge in eighty-nine percent of the episodes.

Positive or Negative Influences Reported by Judge-- Dr. Johnnetta B. Cole. The second judge, Dr. Johnnetta B. Cole, determined all nineteen episodes to be negative influences on self-concept. Dr. Cole made the following statements about some of the shows and episodes:

SHOW I, EPISODE 1

Negative Imageries: The introduction before the appearance of 'Mr. Jackson' is clearly a positive image for the simple reason that an African man is presented as the President of the United States of America. Again, the actual image of this Mr. Jackson is, in fact, positive. He is dressed in a suit as one would expect the President of the United States to be dressed. However, the language and the bodily gestures of this individual certainly do not suggest someone of dignity. Perhaps the most disturbing part of the entire episode is when the imitator of Jesse Jackson, in responding to a question, refers to a phrase that, in fact, is deeply associated with the Jackson bid for the presidency: "Keep hope alive!" In this episode, keeping hope alive refers to freezing Bob Hope. This is hardly a gesture of African-American people.

Likely Influence on Self-Concept: Jesse Jackson, as a presidential candidate, inspired countless African-American children to believe in the possibility that they could one day live in the White House as the head of our nation. This episode picks fun at Jesse Jackson's speech, his ideas, and his mannerisms. Could this be tantamount to picking at the very sense of self that young Black youngsters have of themselves?

SHOW I, EPISODE 3

Negative Imageries: How insulting that the White-American woman should walk on the stage bringing on her back "one member of an endangered species," and it is an African-American man! Thus begins stereotype upon stereotype of Black men.

Likely Influence on Self-Concept: In this episode, an African-American man with an animal is visibly compared. What positive self-concept should any male have of himself after seeing this material?

SHOW I, EPISODE 5

Negative Imageries: This episode involves an African-American man who is under the influence of alcohol, drugs, or both. He is presenting his approach to housing and apparently doing so on television. The first action by the man is a classic old Hollywood stereotype of Black people. Out of ignorance, he makes an electrical connection that goes haywire, and that leads him into all kinds of stereotypical screams and popping of his eyes. Stereotypes turn into pure vulgarity as he bonds two parts of his cardboard house by removing mucous from his nose. Then, references are made to the bathroom as he picks up a jar that has the appearance of urine and feces. These are absolutely and totally negative images of an African-American man.

Likely Influence on Self-Concept: Homelessness is no longer a rare situation among our people. This episode says a large number of African-American, homeless men are drunks, dope addicts, and buffoons. No young person should see this, and certainly no homeless young person. Woe unto his self image if he does!

SHOW II, EPISODE 3

Negative Imageries: An African-American woman in her bathrobe with her hair in rollers is hanging out her window, putting out her wash, and is engaged in gossip about other people in the neighborhood. This is a very negative image of a "two-faced" woman that is saying one thing to them and, subsequently, saying the antithesis to the audience. The woman then turns to one of the most symbolic issues for all of African-American womanhood, that is, our hair. This episode plays directly into the notion of 'good' hair and Native-American blood producing long, silky hair.

Likely Influence on Self-Concept: The woman's last statement is, "You will be fine in this neighborhood; just stay away from nosy, gossiping hens." What a characterization of herself and of African-American women. We must question how our young females will look at themselves when faced with such an episode.

SHOW II, EPISODE 4

Negative Imageries: This episode involves a grown man doing sounds of telephone ringing, pistol shooting, etc. Watching this man go through his antics does not present an image of an African-American man that should be emulated.

Likely Influence on Self-Concept: What disturbs me about this episode is that it implies that African-American men have never grown up. For a source of their self-concept, our young people are not presented African-American men in productive work or positive interactions with their families. They must draw on a grown man acting like a kid!

SHOW II, EPISODE 6

Negative Imageries: This episode involves an African-American family each of whom has a peculiar and deformed head that is in the shape of a buttocks. The interchange in this episode involves double meanings around the family's heads. Interestingly, these people have all the trappings of a middle-class family. Yet, their behavior is so outrageous, their dialogue is so smutty, that we are left with negative images of African-American people.

Likely Influence on Self-Concept: At a time when there is so much concern over the state of African-American families, it is truly sad to think that any young person might have his or her self-concept, as a family member, influenced by this episode. How degrading to see a mother, father, daughter, and son identified in terms of a human buttock.

SHOW III, EPISODE 1

Negative Imageries: This episode involves two African-American men who are Harvard graduates, who come to a country club to apply for jobs as entertainers for the club. The men are portrayed as 'Uncle Toms.' Their behavior is very much that of 'shuffling Negroes.'

Likely Influence on Self-Concept: At the same time that the episode exposes White racism, it also portrays classic Uncle Toms. Hopefully, a young African-American man or woman would not assume that such Uncle Tom behavior is respected by White-Americans or African-Americans. We must ask how this episode would affect a young person's concept about college graduates and their own interest in going to college.

SHOW III, EPISODE 2

Negative Imageries: In this very brief episode, Oprah Winfrey, an African-American woman, who has come to a place of prominence, is presented in unflattering terms. Young African-Americans see so few positive Black-American images in the media. This episode reminds us that when we do have positive role models, they can be presented to us in negative terms.

Likely Influence on Self-Concept: African-American females develop concepts of themselves from multiple sources: family members, what they see and hear in school, and the images around them. The result can be a fundamentally positive or negative self-concept. It is hard to see how this episode would foster, in young Black women, a good sense of other Black women and of themselves.

SHOW III, EPISODE 4

Negative Imageries: This episode involves a school talent show where an African-American parent comes to watch her daughter play the role of a hunk of cheese. Very clearly, this episode advances the stereotype of African-Americans as welfare recipients who are dependent on welfare cheese.

Likely Influence on Self-Concept: This is not what African-American women should use as a behavioral model for mothers, nor should African-American daughters seek to model their behavior after the young person in the episode.

Altogether, Dr. Cole specified nineteen negative influences on self-concept that were one-hundred percent of the episodes.

Positive or Negative Influences Reported by Judge-- Dr. Alvin F. Poussaint. The third judge, Dr. Alvin F. Poussaint, recognized fifteen negative influences on self-concept and four positive influences on self-concept. Some of Dr. Poussaint's analyses are as follows (the numbers under "imageries" correlate with the numbers under "self-concept"):

SHOW I, EPISODE 1

Negative Imageries:
1. A Black man who is President of the United States appears silly and frivolous.
2. The "keep hope alive" slogan is demeaned by presenting a wheelchair-bound 'Bob Hope.'

Likely Influence on Self-Concept:

1. and 2.   The viewer may feel that Reverend Jackson is just stringing them along and that, indeed, there is not much hope. This feeling can demoralize the self.

SHOW I, EPISODE 2

Negative Imageries:
1. Extreme caricatures of soul singers, who sing simple-minded songs, and dress styles. Gives the overall impression of a putdown.
2. The characters are total buffoons.

Likely Influences on Self-Concept:
1. Devalues group culture. May cause viewer to feel negative about his or her group's cultural contributions.

2. Gospel singers and soul singers are people the viewer may feel ashamed of and, therefore, not wish to identify with them.

SHOW I, EPISODE 3

Negative Imageries:

1. White woman carrying Black man on her back like a monkey or ape.
2. Depicts Black male as dangerous.

Likely Influence on Self-Concept:

1. White people dominate and study Blacks as if they are monkeys and apes. May make viewer feel like an "animal."
2. Black men are beast-like and out of control. Gives the impression to the viewer that Blacks are uncivilized.

SHOW I, EPISODE 5

Negative Imageries:

1. Image of a Black homeless man as a dirty, filthy, and drunken bum.
2. Suggests that his penis is an "extension cord."

Likely Influence on Self-Concept:

1. The Black poor are dirty, filthy, non-deserving, and repulsive. No viewer would wish to identify with this man.
2. Reinforces stereotype of the Black male as having a big penis and being a sexual stud. Overemphasizes sexuality and would make a viewer feel that Blacks are less human.

SHOW II, EPISODE 3

Negative Imageries:

A low-income Black woman in hairrows is engaged in malicious and cruel gossip about her neighbors. She presents an image of her neighbors as being dirty and corrupt. Many of the descriptions are salacious and crude.

Likely Influence on Self-Concept:

Profoundly negative image of Black people and the Black poor. This would reinforce stereotypes about Blacks being immoral, dirty, and incompetent. These images weaken the sense of group pride and would deflate the self.

SHOW II, EPISODE 4
Negative Imageries:
The Black performer is portrayed as a fool and buffoon.
Likely Influence on Self-Concept:
Probably mixed influence on self-concept. Part of being a buffoon in this instance may be seen as just part of the act. If being a buffoon is seen as a characteristic of Black people, it would deflate one's sense of self in relationship to group pride.

SHOW II, EPISODE 6
Negative Imageries:
A Black family is presented with buttocks for heads. They also engage in gross behavior, like farting. The children fight and spit at each other. The house smells like "butt and ass."
Likely Influence on Self-Concept:
Essentially says that Blacks are assholes, dirty, and filthy. Reinforces negative stereotypes even though it is done in jest. This would reinforce feelings of unworthiness in a Black person as well as a negative sense of the group.

SHOW IV, EPISODE 5
Negative Imageries:
1. Black kid kicking Black man dressed as a clown in the behind.
2. The Black man/clown puts eggs, milk, and flour on the Black kids' heads to try to whiten them up.
3. The Black man/clown strikes back at the children.
Likely Influence on Self-Concept:
1. This shows a disrespect on the part of children toward Black adults. Indicates a lack of discipline in the Black community. It would have an overall negative effect.
2. It is suggested that in order to make it in society, you have to be White.
3. Shows insecurity and suggests his self-esteem is so low that he has to boost it by attacking other Black people who are 'weaker,' i.e., children.

On the other hand, Dr. Poussaint determined that four episodes projected "positive" influences on self-concept. Two of the episodes and Dr. Poussaint's analyses are as follows:

SHOW III, EPISODE 1

Positive Imageries:

1. Shows open racism in the all-White country club.
2. Tom and Tom make fun of so-called White styles and duplicity.

Likely Influence on Self-Concept:

1. A Black person, although rejected from the club, is merely a victim of discrimination and not inferior.
2. Shows empathy with the problems that Blacks face in dealing with racist White people who are two-faced. This portrayal upholds the basic dignity of the Black person.

SHOW III, EPISODE 3

Positive Imageries:

1. All Blacks don't know how to dance and many need instructions.
2. The 'football team' accepts an effeminate man as its teacher.
3. This episode recognizes that Black football players created the touchdown dance.

Likely Influence on Self-Concept:

1. Gets away from a stereotype that all Blacks have rhythm and know how to dance. It removes the burden of this image and allows the person to feel comfortable with the self regardless of a lack of this ability.
2. Relieves the image that all Black men have to be macho and 'cool' to be acceptable. Shows acceptance of a range of Black styles. This flexibility would support differences as being okay and boost group pride.
3. May be mixed. There would be pride in Black people because of this cultural achievement. However, if a Black person saw this type of dancing as demeaning, it might reinforce embarrassment about the Black group and damage the self-concept.

Once more, Dr. Poussaint specified fifteen negative influences on self-concept and four positive influences on self-concept. The negative influences of self-concept were reported by this judge in seventy-nine percent of the episodes.

Conclusion for Subquestion I. All judges unitedly concurred on thirteen out of nineteen episodes that were likely to have negative influences on self-concepts of young African-American adults. None of the judges unitedly concurred that any episodes were likely to have positive influences on self-concepts of young African-American adults.

The judges' data explain that the episodes are likely to have negative influences on self-perceptions of the young African-American viewers. For reiteration, some of the judges' statements pertaining to the "likely influences on self-concept" are as follows:

- Dr. Kenneth B. Clark: "Young Blacks could see themselves as being funny in any serious political position; therefore, a likely influence on self-concept would be negative."

- Dr. Johnnetta B. Cole: "African-American females develop concepts of themselves from multiple sources: family members, what they see and hear in school, and the images around them. The result can be a fundamentally positive or negative self-concept. It is hard to see how this episode would foster, in young Black women, a good sense of other Black women and of themselves."

- Dr. Alvin F. Poussaint: "Reinforces stereotype of the Black male as having a big penis and being a sexual stud. Overemphasizes sexuality and would make a viewer feel that Blacks are less human."

It is clear that the episodes' reiterative message is one which posits that African-Americans' behaviors, attitudes, and values are negative. It is reasonable, then, to conclude that the episodes were viewed by the judges to have negative influences on self.

Subquestion II: What Does Each Judge Consider to be the Major Likely Influence on Self?

Dr. Kenneth B. Clark. Dr. Clark's common theme relative to negative influences on self was that "stereotypes of various sorts" obstruct young adult African-Americans' possibilities to "emerge with a positive self-image from almost any one of the episodes."

For example, in Show I, Episode 3, Dr. Clark states that the negative imagery of the character's role "is potentially subhuman, if not almost animalistic." Because of this negative imagery, there is "a disturbing negative influence on self-concept depicting Blacks as subhuman."

Dr. Clark's data unequivocally assert that stereotypes are the major likely influences on self in the episodes.

Dr. Johnnetta B. Cole. Dr. Cole expressed that these "spoofs on African-American behavior can and do influence how African-Americans see themselves." For example, in Show II, Episode 6, Dr. Cole stated that the episode has "an African-American family, each of whom has a peculiar and deformed head that is in the shape of a buttocks. . . . It is truly sad to think that any young person might have his or her self-concept as a family member influenced by this episode. How degrading to see a mother, father, daughter, and son identified in terms of a human buttock."

Dr. Cole's data unequivocally specifies that degrading "spoofs" on African-Americans are the major likely influences on self in the episodes.

Dr. Alvin F. Poussaint. Dr. Poussaint's common thought about influences on self was how demeaning stereotypes can "deflate" the self. For example, in Show II, Episode 3, Dr. Poussaint stated that "a low-income Black woman in hairrows is engaged in malicious, cruel gossip about her neighbors. She presents an image of her neighbors as being dirty and corrupt. Many of the descriptions are salacious and crude. . . . This is a profoundly negative image of Black people and the Black poor. This would reinforce stereotypes about Blacks being immoral, dirty, and incompetent. These images weaken the sense of group pride and would deflate the self."

Dr. Poussaint's data unequivocally affirms that demeaning stereotypes are the major likely influences on self in the episodes. **Conclusion for Subquestion II.** The three judges, Dr. Kenneth B. Clark, Dr. Johnnetta B. Cole, and Dr. Alvin F. Poussaint, overwhelmingly agreed that degrading stereotypes are the major likely influences on self in the episodes.

The degrading stereotypes pertaining to behaviors, attitudes, values, social and economical status sets apart African-Americans from other ethnic people. Furthermore, it is reasonable to conclude that the episodes' reiterative message is one that establishes that African-Americans appear to be negatively 'different' than other ethnic people and, therefore, inferior to other ethnic people.

Subquestion III: What Likely Influences Were Identified by All of the Judges in the Selected Episodes?

The three judges, Dr. Kenneth B. Clark, Dr. Johnnetta B. Cole, and Dr. Alvin F. Poussaint, identified degrading stereotypes as the likely influences in the selected episodes. To support this statement, I will list three episodes per judge.

Dr. Kenneth B. Clark. Dr. Clark identified the following degrading stereotypes as likely influences on self:

*   Show I, Episode 5: The entire episode is a negative image. It destructively humorizes drug addicts, the homeless, and the poor; it disgustingly pokes fun at economic and racial tragedy.
*   Show II, Episode 1: A Black man is portrayed as a silly-looking clown who curses, strikes women, and has spent "eight years in prison."
*   Show II, Episode 3: There is stereotypical joking toward home, family, poverty, and especially children ("crack addict in the making").

Dr. Johnnetta B. Cole. Dr. Cole identified the following degrading stereotypes as likely influences on self:

*   Show III, Episode 1: This episode involves two African-American men who are Harvard graduates, who come to a country club to apply for jobs as entertainers for the

club. The two African-American men are portrayed as 'Uncle Toms.' Their behavior is very much that of 'shuffling Negroes.' What a negative image!

• Show III, Episode 2: In this very brief episode, Oprah Winfrey, an African-American woman, who has come to a place of prominence, is presented in unflattering terms. Young African-Americans see so few positive Black-American images in the media. This episode reminds us that when we do have positive role models, they can be presented to us in negative terms.

• Show III, Episode 3: In this episode, a football coach brings in an African-American man to work with a losing football team. He is the stereotype of a gay man. The image of the gay man is not a positive one. . . . Indeed, sports have been one of the few avenues that young people, particularly African-American young men, see for their advancement. In this episode, a very cherished pastime for many African-American male youths are belittled and distorted. In the African-American communities, it is important to struggle against homophobia, but this is not the way to wage that struggle. Any gay young person would certainly not gain a positive self-concept from this episode.

Dr. Alvin F. Poussaint. Dr. Poussaint identified the following degrading stereotypes as likely influences on self:

• Show I, Episode 1:
   1. Extreme caricatures of Reverend Jackson's rhyming and jingle style speech. A Black man who is President of the United States appears silly and frivolous.
   2. The "keep hope alive" slogan is demeaned by presenting a wheelchair-bound 'Bob Hope.' The viewer may feel that Reverend Jackson is just stringing them along and that, indeed, there is not much hope. This feeling can demoralize the self.

• Show I, Episode 2:
   1. Extreme caricatures of soul singers and dress styles, who sing simple-minded songs. Gives the overall impression of a putdown. Devalues group culture.

May cause viewer to feel negative about his or her group's cultural contributions.

2. The characters are total buffoons. Gospel singers and soul singers are people the viewer may feel ashamed of and, therefore, not wish to identify with them.

• Show I, Episode 5:
1. Image of a Black homeless man as a dirty, filthy, and drunken bum. The Black poor are perceived to be dirty, filthy, non-deserving, and repulsive. No viewer would wish to identify with this man.

2. Suggests that his penis is an extension cord. Reinforces stereotype of the Black male as having a big penis and being a sexual stud. Overemphasizes sexuality and would make a viewer feel that Blacks are less human.

Conclusion for Subquestion III. None of the judges jointly agreed on any of the nineteen episodes having positive influences on self-concept. Of the three judges, two judges expressed that some episodes had positive influences on self-concept. One judge, Dr. Kenneth B. Clark, declared two episodes to have positive influences on self-concept. Dr. Alvin F. Poussaint specified four episodes to have positive influences on self-concept. However, Dr. Clark's and Dr. Poussaint's episodes were not the same positive episodes. Dr. Johnnetta B. Cole stated that all of the nineteen episodes had negative influences on self-concept.

The data indicate that most of the episodes are negative; therefore, it is reasonable to suggest that the episodes are likely to have negative influences on self-perceptions of young adult African-American television viewers. This concludes the data analysis for Question 1.

QUESTION 2: WHAT POSSIBLE INFLUENCE DO
PARTICULAR TELEVISION IMAGERIES HAVE ON
SELF-PERCEPTIONS OF SELECTED YOUNG
ADULT AFRICAN-AMERICANS?

I composed three subquestions that will guide the analysis
relative to Question 2 ("What possible influences do particular
television imageries have on self-perceptions of selected young
adult African-Americans?").

**Subquestion I: Did the Interviewees Perceive the Episodes to be
Positive or Negative Relating to Their Self-Perceptions as
African-Americans?**

The ten interviewees' responses are demonstrated on the
Researcher's Data Matrix (see Table 3).

The interviewees consisted of five African-American
women and five African-American men who were between the
ages of eighteen to twenty-five. I asked interviewees to view
four television shows that contained a total of nineteen
episodes. Each interviewee viewed the identical shows that
were given to the judges. After each episode, I orally questioned
the interviewees. Moreover, the interviewees represented
diverse economical and educational histories. Again, refer to
Appendix C ("Personal History Form" and "Profiles of
Interviewees") for specific information on interviewees.

[Note: Throughout this chapter, all episodes that were
determined to be positive *and* negative will be known as
hybrids.]

Interviewees' Responses to Episodes. The following presents
each interviewee's response to the episodes:

- **Leroy:** Leroy perceived ten episodes to be positive and
  nine episodes to be negative.
- **Keri:** Keri perceived five episodes to be positive and
  nine episodes to be negative. However, Keri perceived
  five episodes to be hybrids.

Table 3
Researcher's Data Matrix

SHOW	EPISODE	1 Leroy	2 Keri	3 John	4 Ahmed	5 Elizabeth	6 Barbara	7 Lisa	8 Thelma	9 David	10 Gordon
I	1	+	+	+	+/-	-	+	+	-	+	-
I	2	+	-	-	-	-	-	-	+/-	-	-
I	3	-	+/-	+	-	-	-	-	-	+/-	-
I	4	+	+/-	-	-	-	-	-	-	+/-	-
I	5	-	-	+/-	-	-	-	+	+/-	-	-
II	1	+	-	+	+/-	-	-	+	-	+	+/-
II	2	+	-	+	-	-	+	+	+	+	-
II	3	+	-	-	-	+/-	-	-	-	+/-	-
II	4	-	+	-	-	+	-	+	+	+	-
II	6	-	+	+	-	-	-	+	+	-	+
III	1	-	+/-	-	-	+/-	-	-	-	-	-
III	2	+	+	-	-	-	+	+	+/-	-	-
III	3	-	+/-	-	-	-	+	-	+	-	+/-
III	4	-	-	-	-	-	+/-	-	-	-	-
III	5	-	+/-	+	-	+/-	+/-	+	+	-	+
IV	1	+	-	-	-	-	+/-	+	+/-	+/-	-
IV	2	-	-	-	+/-	-	-	-	+/-	-	+/-
IV	4	+	-	+	-	-	-	+/-	-	-	-
IV	5	+	+	+	-	-	-	+	+/-	+/-	-

+	=	Positive
-	=	Negative
+/-	=	Positive/Negative (Hybrid)

- **John:** John perceived eight episodes to be positive and ten episodes to be negative. John considered one show to be hybrid.
- **Ahmed:** Ahmed perceived sixteen episodes to be negative and three episodes to be hybrids.
- **Elizabeth:** Elizabeth perceived one episode to be positive, fifteen episodes to be negative, and three episodes to be hybrids.
- **Barbara:** Barbara perceived four episodes to be positive, twelve episodes to be negative, and three episodes to be hybrids.
- **Lisa:** Lisa perceived ten episodes to be positive, eight episodes to be negative, and one episode to be a hybrid.
- **Thelma:** Thelma perceived five episodes to be positive, eight episodes to be negative, and six episodes to be hybrids.
- **David:** David perceived four episodes to be positive, ten episodes to be negative, and five episodes to be hybrids.
- **Gordon:** Gordon perceived two episodes to be positive, fourteen episodes to be negative, and three episodes to be hybrids.

Conclusion for Subquestion I. With the exception of Ahmed, all interviewees perceived some episodes to be positive. All interviewees perceived some episodes to be negative. With the exception of Leroy, all interviewees perceived some episodes to be hybrids.

Because there were ten interviewees and nineteen episodes, there were one hundred ninety answers. Collectively, the interviewees identified forty-nine episodes to be positive, one hundred eleven episodes to be negative, and thirty episodes to be hybrids. In other words, twenty-six percent of the interviewees' responses to the episodes were positive, fifty-eight percent of the interviewees' responses to the episodes were negative, and sixteen percent of the interviewees' responses were hybrid.

Subquestion II: What Were the Positive and Negative Influences on the Episodes as Reported by the Interviewees?

The following presents the positive and negative influences on the episodes as reported by the interviewees:

- **Leroy**: Leroy perceived more episodes to have positive influences than negative influences. Leroy did not perceive any episodes to be hybrids.
- **Keri**: Keri perceived more episodes to have negative influences than positive influences. Moreover, Keri had an equal number of positive and hybrid perceptions of the episodes.
- **John**: John perceived more episodes to have negative influences than positive influences. John identified one episode to be hybrid.
- **Ahmed**: Ahmed did not perceive any episodes to have sole positive influences. He identified all episodes to have negative influences except three hybrids.
- **Elizabeth**: Elizabeth perceived more episodes to have negative influences than positive influences. She identified three episodes to be hybrids.
- **Barbara**: Barbara perceived more episodes to have negative influences than positive influences. Additionally, she identified three shows to be hybrids.
- **Lisa**: Lisa perceived more episodes to have positive influences than negative influences. Also, Lisa identified one episode to be hybrid.
- **Thelma**: Thelma perceived more episodes to have negative influences than positive influences. She identified six episodes to be hybrids.
- **David**: David perceived more episodes to have negative influences than positive influences. He identified five hybrid episodes.
- **Gordon**: Gordon perceived more episodes to have negative influences than positive influences. He identified three hybrid episodes.

Summary of Positive and Negative Influences on the Episodes as Reported by the Interviewees. Two interviewees perceived more episodes to have positive influences than negative influences. Eight interviewees perceived more episodes to have negative influences. One interviewee perceived all episodes to have negative influences except for some hybrids; and nine interviewees perceived some episodes to be hybrids.

Additionally, none of the interviewees perceived all of the episodes to have positive influences. None of the interviewees perceived all of the episodes to have negative influences.

The following presents statements by the interviewees of positive and negative influences in particular episodes:

• **Leroy:** Leroy made the following statements relative to some of the ten episodes he perceived to have "positive influences":

Show I, Episode 1:

I don't see anything wrong with this episode. You know everybody's laughing at all creeds, colors, religions. There isn't anything wrong with it. . . . It just doesn't touch me in any way. That episode is just human. That's all, it doesn't affect me.

Show I, Episode 2:

It doesn't affect me; it doesn't affect me. The episode as a whole is just humor. That's all I see – that's humor, that's humor.

Show II, Episode 1:

That episode, yeah, the character is saying it like it is. He's tired of taking all that's dished out; he's tired, real tired. Yeah, I like this one. This one was great.

Show II, Episode 3:

It's funny. A lot of that takes place. . . . In this episode, I guess she is on welfare. Evidently she is in poverty – so-called poor class. When I saw her, I just laughed because anybody that takes that much of their time to be in somebody's business, when they have so much of their business to tend to . . . you only laugh at those people. This is just funny. It takes place.

Show III, Episode 2:
This episode doesn't touch me. It's humor. Oprah Winfrey's on so many diets. You see her one year skinny and the next year fat again. . . . Like I always said, if you're fat, God has gifted you with either being real cute or real talented.

The following statements were made by Leroy relative to some of the nine episodes he considered to have "negative influences":

Show I, Episode 3:
Yeah, this episode touches me. . . . That's the typical stereotype corporate America has about young Black men. That their pants are drooping. It's what on the inside that counts, you know, not just clothing. That's what White America thinks about all young Blacks. . . . It's that image of clothing.

Show I, Episode 5:
This episode here, this one is different. Homelessness here in the city is a big problem. As you see with this episode, even though I am laughing, I see the extent he has to go through to provide for himself. . . . That's not even a Black issue, that's of all people. . . . It's humor, but, at the same time, it's touching. . . . I know that I'm a long way from a cardboard box, I know that, so I'm going to . . . this episode this. . . . Even though I never lived in a cardboard box, I know I wouldn't want to live in one.

Show III, Episode 3:
There's a stigma attached to all Black males being good in sports. In sports, you don't use your brain as much as you would in an executive position with a big corporation. . . . Too much of America has perceived Black males as just being too athletic. . . . The day we're born, we're bouncing basketballs. The homosexual man, I mean, at that level, he was a professional. Just because he was gay, the people didn't look at his professionalism.

Conclusion for Leroy. Of the episodes that Leroy perceived to have positive influences, his common theme was: "It doesn't affect me; it is just funny."

Of the episodes that Leroy perceived to have negative influences, his common themes were stereotypes of African-American males, such as Leroy's references to an image of clothing for young African-Americans as "a stigma attached to all Black males being good in sports."

• **Keri**: The following statements were made by Keri relative to some of the five episodes she perceived to have "positive influences":
Show I, Episode 1:
Even though he's saying it in a joking way, I understand what he is saying. I feel that we, as a people, have a talent to imitate or to make a joke out of things, but at the same time understand that reality behind it . . . to be able to laugh at the same time.
Show II, Episode 4:
The character that was portrayed, the scene itself, and the surroundings were positive. He had on a suit. He looked presentable. . . . I would consider it to be positive because the character was supposed to be a sound . . . because this is his type of art. Instead of an instrument, his mouth is the instrument.
Show IV, Episode 5:
I'm never in agreement with this character, but this time I can relate to him because this girl was trying to help him – but to satisfy herself more so. I just picture myself in that situation right now, because from what I've heard from my friends, our Black males feel if they can't hold onto a relationship, it is because their girlfriends are always trying to change them to be someone they want him to be. The male character was positive to the point that he didn't allow himself to be changed despite the fact that he was in love with her.
The following statements were made by Keri relative to some of the nine episodes she perceived to have "negative influences":
Show I, Episode 2:
I guess they are doing it for a laugh, basically, but it doesn't look good for us because this is the stereotypical view anyway.
Show I, Episode 5:
First of all, he's a bum in the street. Apparently, he's an alcoholic and, apparently, he likes where he is because he's adding onto his home that he has on the street. . . . I'm around them constantly and I know they all are not like that. You

might find a few that somehow got lost along the way, but I haven't seen any that bad off. . . . I don't know whether he's trying to exaggerate a point to prove that there's more to life than what you see here or trying to draw more people to be like that. . . . I think that if you instill more positive, then that'll stick with people more so than the negative.

Show II, Episode 1:

I don't like this character because he portrays a clown; and as a child, you always think fun and games when you see a clown, but not this clown. . . . He's supposed to have this type of relationship with children, but he's cruel to them and he uses profanity.

Show III, Episode 4:

She wasn't presentable at all; you don't have to be rich to look decent or have an abundance of money to look presentable. She didn't look clean, her hair wasn't combed. . . . I feel as if people who watch this might see this as a point against me as an African-American woman trying to make it. It might be a negative hanging over my head. . . . That's one against me, already, to be portrayed in that manner. . . . We're portrayed as being from the projects, eating the government cheese.

Conclusion for Keri. Of the episodes that Keri perceived to have positive influences, her common theme was: "Understand the reality behind the joke, to be able to laugh at the same time."

Of the episodes that Keri perceived to have negative influences, her common themes were stereotypes of African-Americans, such as African-Americans being portrayed as cruel, profane, and "eating the government cheese."

• **John:** The following statements were made by John relative to some of the eight episodes he perceived to have "positive influences":

Show I, Episode 3:

It was positive in its own right. What they basically showed were the differences between two classes, two races: the B-Boy style or the hoods and the White Americans. It was positive as far as seeing the B-Boys. . . . If I was with my peers, it would be totally acceptable because that's the way my peers dress. If we were with an older crowd, they would probably think that it was more negative. . . . He's a young Black American male. He does the things that young Black American males do. And most older people tend to want you to steer away from that and want you to act like corporate America or White America. Sit up there with a suit and a tie and be phoney.

Show II, Episode 1:

He wouldn't succumb or lower himself to any type of standards that they portray Black Americans doing. To me, he's positive because he was a strong real man. . . . It seemed like no matter what the hardships are, he still had his dignity, his pride, and everything. . . . You know, as far as wealth, he probably wouldn't do what corporate America or White America would want you to do. . . . It seemed like he had pride in himself and he was a strong-willed individual and that's the way I pictured myself. . . . Even though he was portraying a clown, still he wasn't a clown. His actions were not that of a clown. The costume really had no bearing on it--no bearing. It was just an outfit.

Show II, Episode 6:

I couldn't see anyone trying to relate that to Black America or any type of racial group as far as the image they portrayed there. It was comedy. It was funny.

The following statements were made by John relative to some of the ten episodes he perceived to have "negative influences":

Show III, Episode 1:

I mean that was low. The things they had to do in there. I mean, it was like they were not conscious of what they were doing. . . . It was bad. I didn't like that at all. . . . I'm just glad that I'm not like that. I'm not that blind.

Show III, Episode 4:

You know, with the mother and the kid, the way that they acted; the government cheese; the family. They didn't have any positive portrayals of Black-Americans in any of the characters. . . . You might not notice it consciously, but, subconsciously, it's always implanted that Blacks are always on welfare. Black people are always eating the government cheese.

Show IV, Episode 1:

Well, with the sergeant or the recruiter, I felt it was bad because even though the guy was a bum, he came in to serve his country. That might not have been the reason; but as a recruiter, if somebody wants to come in and sign up for the Army, you are supposed to take them. But the recruiter didn't want to take him because he was a bum, I guess. . . . It can be another devastating blow to a person like that because they have been let down so many times in life, that when they try to do something that's good . . . you know . . . that's another put down. . . . He needed money; he went to the Army where they could provide him with food or a place to sleep.

Conclusion for John. Of the episodes that John perceived to have positive influences, his common themes were: strong identification with his peers, pride about being a Black person, and "It was funny."

Of the episodes that John perceived to have negative influences, his common themes were stereotypes of African-American people, such as African-Americans being depicted as welfare recipients and "always eating the government cheese."

• **Ahmed:** The following statements were made by Ahmed relative to some of the sixteen episodes he perceived to have "negative influences." Ahmed did not perceive any episodes to have sole "positive influences."

Show I, Episode 2:

I noticed that the episodes, in general, seemed to make me feel different about myself, depending on whether they are enjoyable or not. I didn't really find this one to be funny. It just seemed poor in taste.

Show I, Episode 3:

If they are going to make some kind of fun about the B-Boy .-.-. the way that they sort of brought him out like he was some creature for the show . . . that part of it really bothered me. Almost referring to him as a thing versus a man. I find that African-American people in this country in general have always been looked upon more as creatures than individuals and people like everyone else.

Show II, Episode 2:

So again, those myths about sexual virility and manhood based on sexual activity, again, I think that enforces those negative images, negative stereotypes. . . . I think this sort of pushes the negative sexual myths about African males.

Show III, Episode 3:

Promoting the stereotype of welfare mothers, children, teenage pregnancy . . . it shows that our people, as a whole, really don't want to work for anything. We'd rather just stay at home all day long and just gossip, watch T.V., and just receive whatever free money we can get. That didn't set well with me at all.

Conclusion for Ahmed. Ahmed did not perceive any episodes to have positive influences. Of the episodes that Ahmed perceived to have negative influences, his common themes were stereotypes of African-American males, such as African-American males being portrayed as "creatures" rather "than individuals" and "myths about sexual virility."

• **Elizabeth**: The following statements were made by Elizabeth relative to the sole episode she perceived to have a "positive influence":

Show II, Episode 4:

For once I can say, my race wasn't a factor. I just thought that this was really cute. I didn't really feel any negativity. I didn't think about that at all.

The following statements were made by Elizabeth relative to some of the fifteen episodes she perceived to have "negative influences":

Show I, Episode 5:

I think the first thing that comes into my mind is that we are relegated to the basic roles. We are either drunkards, we're from the lower dregs of society, we're ignorant, you know, those types of things. I've been fortunate enough to know who I am, so when I don't see positive images of myself, I don't internalize that. . . . For a period of time, I did not really find myself as attractive. I rarely saw anyone who really looked like me on television. . . . You really don't see any role models on T.V. Once again, you have all these negative portrayals and you internalize those things, especially if you come from an environment that is full of negativity and you don't really see a way out. So it really depends on your experiences and how you decipher those messages that come in.

Show II, Episode 1:

A lot of things were going through my mind when I was watching it. Number one, the theme that the Black man is always a clown, never taken seriously. The second thing, the word "bitch," again. . . . Now people don't care about women. . . . You know, they are just self-serving. . . . When I was at Penn State, which is in Western Pennsylvania, in a very remote town . . . there aren't any Blacks there. So, some people from these small towns, that's all they have to identify – programs like this. So when they see me, it's like, "Oh my God, I can't believe it." And I say, "Why can't you believe it?" Because this is all they see on T.V.

Show II, Episode 2:

Relationships, it always seems to dwell on sex or inadequacy.

Show IV, Episode 5:

He took his frustration out on her violently. . . . Society as a whole has condoned violence against women.

Conclusion for Elizabeth. The episode that Elizabeth perceived to have a positive influence had one common theme, that was, neutral imagery. For Elizabeth, this episode was a neutral imagery because "race wasn't a factor."

Of the episodes that Elizabeth perceived to have negative influences, her common themes were stereotypes of African-Americans, such as African-Americans being portrayed as "drunkards . . . the lower dregs of society and ignorant." Additionally, African-American men were depicted as being disrespectful of African-American women by referring to the women as "bitches."

- **Barbara:** The following statements were made by Barbara relative to some of the four episodes she perceived to have "positive influences":

Show III, Episode 2:
That episode is positive for people watching it . . . because it does express being on drugs is bad.
Show III, Episode 3:
The choreographer wanted to keep them in shape so it could help them with their football. So I thought it was positive, even though he was a homosexual. . . . Also, it made me feel happy to see that teamwork was being done.

The following statements were made by Barbara relative to some of the twelve episodes she perceived to be "negative":
Show I, Episode 2:
It was negative because they don't speak proper English and they are a bit foolish. . . . Younger people looking at that might say, "Hey, all I have to do is say 'ain't' and I can be a star." I think that is not the image I want for Black people.
Show I, Episode 3:
The way he was brought in as an animal, the language, his posture. He was like a species of some sort. That could be looked upon as though the White man is trying to put us in a corner and say that is what all Black males are like.
Show IV, Episode 2:
It made me feel that in a relationship, I should have open communication with my spouse. Then I wouldn't have this type of problem. I know I'm going to talk to my husband about different situations not to have to go to a counselor and beat him into doing right.
Show IV, Episode 4:
It made me feel that I'm fortunate to be where I am; being able to go to places that I have been and not have to pretend to be something else or act like that . . . pretending, trying to rhyme. I want to be myself regardless of what is around me. Rich or poor, I'm always myself.

Conclusion for Barbara. Of the episodes that Barbara perceived to have positive influences, her common themes were to be anti-drugs and to participate in team work. Two quotes relative to Barbara's themes were: "Being on drugs is bad" and "It made me feel happy to see that teamwork was being done."

Of the episodes that Barbara perceived to have negative influences, her common theme was negative imagery of African-

Americans, such as African-Americans being portrayed as "animals" and "not speaking proper English."

• **Lisa:** The following statements were made by Lisa relative to some of the ten episodes she perceived to have "positive influences":

Show I, Episode 5:
The person in the skit appeared to be homeless and probably an alcoholic. . . . I think he just portrayed him in what he felt would be positive. He didn't really try to bring down the character. That's just what he has seen. I think he just did it for fun, for a laugh.

Show II, Episode 1:
I think he was trying to bring across a message that some people end up like that when they have been put down so long in society. . . . I feel that he was trying to bring across a message that he can do it funny, do it in a comical skit. I don't think he was saying anything negative about African-Americans.

Show II, Episode 6:
I don't think they were portraying any particular race. They just wanted to do something funny. And they did it in a funny way. It was positive. I didn't see anything negative or stereotypical about it.

Show IV, Episode 1:
This one was kind of hard. He was positive, I guess. He wasn't portraying a positive person. His life wasn't together and he really didn't know what he wanted. But it wasn't because he was trying and somebody was pushing him back. He just wants to get over. And he portrayed that in a positive way as a person that just wants to get over. And the person in the Army, he portrayed a positive image, also. He didn't want anything to do with the other guy. I think he felt like he was a better man than the other guy. He was still portrayed in a positive way, though.

Show IV, Episode 5:
I felt good because he was trying to say that he had been put down for so long, that he wasn't going to go with the normal ways of society. He was going to do his own thing and make it work for him.

The following statements were made by Lisa relative to
some of the eight episodes she perceived to have "negative
influences":
Show I, Episode 2:
This was really funny, but I thought it was kind of
negative. It was negative because I think they elaborated too
much on the bad language. . . . A lot of people think that as
Black-Americans we can't express ourselves or we can't speak.
Show II, Episode 3:
It was funny, but negative only because it portrayed women
in general--maybe not just Black women, but women in general
as just gossipy, hanging out the window, talking. . . . I don't
want to be like that; because once you see it on television, it's
not a positive thing. You may think to yourself, "I don't want to
turn out like that." It made me feel good because I know that's
not what I do, but it made me think there are a lot of women
who do that.
Conclusion for Lisa. Of the episodes that Lisa perceived to
have positive influences, her common theme was: "I don't
really think it's negative; I think he just did it for fun, for a
laugh."
Of the episodes that Lisa perceived to have negative
influences, her common themes were stereotypes of African-
Americans, such as African-Americans being incapable of
articulating the English language and "gossipy" women.

• **Thelma**: The following statements were made by
Thelma relative to some of the five episodes she perceived to
have "positive influences":
Show II, Episode 2:
This particular episode didn't really bother me. I don't see
anything wrong with it. . . . It's good to talk about your
problems.
Show II, Episode 6:
In our everyday life, we don't see unordinary people and
you see unordinary people on this show and how they live. Like
he told his son, "Don't let it bother you, just turn the other
cheek." It's just to be taken as a joke. That's how I thought . . . to
make it more funny.

Show III, Episode 3:

They all stuck together. Even though they didn't like the homosexual, they let him teach the class. So it helped to win the game. . . . We can all work together if we try.

The following statements were made by Thelma relative to some of the eight episodes she perceived to have "negative influences":

Show I, Episode 1:

When you see something like this, it's like, "Oh, they're making a joke out of it." So when the White man sees it, he says, "If they are going to make a joke about it, then we can make a joke about it, too."

Show I, Episode 4:

Like I said, well that one deals with minorities in general. And when you look at something like that, you feel, well, is that how they act? The way the women were dressed, used a lot of vulgarity, that really wasn't called for.

Show II, Episode 3:

O.K., you see a Black person. You know she is trying to do something for herself, but, yet, she's not helping anybody else because all she does is talk about them all day long. It's uncalled for. . . . It makes me feel bad because you wonder, "Well, how do I know that someone is not talking about me?" She doesn't know what the other people are doing when she's not looking. She just knows when she's watching them.

Show III, Episode 3:

It made me feel like not wanting to be around too many Black people because they look Black on the outside; but when you get to them on the inside, they are really White.

Conclusion for Thelma. Of the episodes that Thelma perceived to have positive influences, her common theme was: "It's just to be taken as a joke."

Of the episodes that Thelma perceived to have negative influences, her common themes were negative imageries of African-Americans, such as African-Americans being depicted as using vulgar language, nosy, gossipy women, and a silly, unserious politician.

• **David:** The following statements were made by David relative to some of the four episodes he perceived to have "positive influences":

Show II, Episode 1:

Even though they did it in an awkward manner, they showed how the Black person has been programmed to self-destruct by not having an education. So everything he was saying was true. They just did it in a round about way. They did it in a joking manner, but it was serious.

Show II, Episode 2:

It showed that sometimes a man will harbor frustrations and take it out on a woman. That's real and many men don't want to deal with it. And the fact that they brought it up shows that they are trying to educate the audience. . . . I feel that after viewing this episode, that you have to be sensitive to a woman.

Show II, Episode 4:

I felt good about myself because I see this in a different way. Number one, it shows that a Black man is aware of what's going on around him. Number two, that we are talented just like anybody else; and when we put our minds to it, we can do whatever we want.

The following statements were made by David relative to ten episodes he perceived to have "negative influences":

Show III, Episode 1:

This plays the worse stereotype of all. . . . You have to think White to belong to a White social club. Also, it showed a Black man as the butler. . . . They tried to use comedy, but they chose the wrong type of issue considering the racism that we have to deal with in America.

Show III, Episode 2:

It is making fun of a heavyset Black woman. Heavyset Black women have been known as the "mammy" type of people. You know, they always took care of everybody. . . . It plays out the basic stereotype. I guess some Black people could see themselves as this. . . . What's the purpose? It wasn't that funny. It was embarrassing.

Show III, Episode 4:
It didn't make me feel good because it shows that sometimes we're out here being laid off from our jobs. I didn't like the fact that they showed the Black female with man-like thick features, the oversized butt, the chest protruding. It goes back to the manly-type Black female that Hollywood portrayed back in the 1930s and 1940s and 1950s. . . . This segment gives the impression that the female is just supposed to stay home and be barefoot and pregnant. . . . I didn't feel good about myself after viewing this episode because it played all the general stereotypes.

Show IV, Episode 4:
It makes it seem like the Black man thinks of her only as a "hoe" and the "B-word." It also goes with the image of the real fat gold chains and goes on the stereotype that most Black rappers are ignorant. Some are, but not all of them; but it portrays that stereotype . . . that we can't do a song without using profanity or degrading our counterparts. . . . You don't feel too good about yourself knowing that we are perceived as the ones that are always degrading our own women. You know that we also must swear, curse, and do everything else that's considered negative.

Conclusion for David. Of the episodes that David perceived to have positive influences, his common theme was: "They did it in a joking manner, but they were serious."

Of the episodes that David perceived to have negative influences, his common themes were stereotypes of African-Americans, such as African-American women with "manlike features," the "stereotype that most Black rappers are ignorant," and a Black man featured as a butler.

• **Gordon:** The following statements were made by Gordon relative to the sole two episodes he perceived to have "positive influences":

Show II, Episode 6:
Gee, I saw it as, I guess, humor. That's about it. I really didn't see anything racist in it, except the fact that throughout all these skits, this is the only skit that's been portrayed with a family; a family setting – a mother, father, and children.

That's the only thing that's startling. The fact that that's the only time that they showed a family.

Show III, Episode 5:

Number one, there is an African-American female teacher. I like that. And she knew what to do when the fire marshal came out. . . . It shows that Black people are intelligent and they know what to do. They aren't just sitting in class and learning nothing. . . . I saw myself able to learn in that classroom, able to learn in that atmosphere.

The following statements were made by Gordon relative to some of the fourteen episodes he perceived to have "negative influences":

Show I, Episode 1:

Well, I saw it to be negative because it was on national television. When you look at it, it's supposed to be in a joking manner. When you joke about Black leaders, politicians, or Black activists, it's perceived to be negative. How can you look at somebody who's trying to better our community and make jokes about them as a Black person? . . . When I first looked at it, I basically saw humor in it. But it's not humorous because you look at "Hope Alive" and they talked about Bob Hope. When Jesse Jackson talks about "Hope Alive," he's talking about something serious. He's talking about a hope of a brighter America in terms of domestic needs, racial needs, and sexual needs or whatever. To make fun of what is sort of undermining his whole campaign because his campaign relies on "keep hope alive" . . . I believe that a Black person should not undermine him or his coalition in any shape or form.

Show I, Episode 3:

I didn't like that episode; that's the stereotype of every single Black male American. The reason why I didn't like that is because Black people are portrayed as hoodlums. You see them on the media going into cop cars; you see them being arrested; when you see burglaries or what have you. . . . I know a lot of people who don't see themselves as this, but they act like this. And when they actually see themselves like this, they stop and think, "Gee, do I really act like this? Do I really portray this type of person?" It's really bad, man. That's not the way every Black person acts.

Show I, Episode 4:
Very negative, extremely negative. Because it brought in every single stereotype that's brought up on the Hispanic culture. I don't think that's right. The machismo man; the woman that's weak-minded and always staying with him; always hot-blooded and always having sex; the gossiping within that whole establishment . . . I felt badly because African-Americans were playing that role. . . . I would feel badly talking to someone of Latin origin about this episode because that's totally disgraceful.

Show I, Episode 5:
I'd feel bad because homelessness is a serious problem. That's something serious and it shouldn't be joked about like what they did on that television episode. I mean, homelessness is a serious problem, and they're making fun of it. . . . Whenever they do shows on the homeless, they show Black males. I think it's a negative image of Black males.

Show III, Episode 1:
As an African-American who plans to enter the corporate field, I don't want to see myself end up like those two Toms, the two Black people portrayed in that episode . . . and it makes me feel bad because I see two Black people who have done something with their lives and they're collaborating with Whites. They think that they are part of the White culture and they've forgotten about their Black heritage. That's upsetting to me. And another thing that's upsetting to me is the fact that you look at that and you think that, well, I guess it's perceived that every Black person who's making it in the corporate world is selling out themselves. And that's simply not true. Every Black person who's making it in the corporate world is *not* selling out themselves. They're just able to hold that position and get a job. It doesn't mean that they have turned into, as that portrays, Uncle Toms. They're just being able to make it in the corporate world.

Show III, Episode 2:
I saw it as racist because there's a stereotype about Blacks liking pork and fried foods. And it showed Oprah Winfrey, an African-American woman, who's doing something with her life, in a negative outlook that I didn't like. If anything, we

should be happy to see that she is doing something with her life, rather than trying to take it away from her. It's a racial thing with pork and fried foods that Blacks have. It's just supporting that big myth that Blacks, all they eat is pork, and that made me feel bad. I don't like the way African-American people are perceived when it comes to those stereotypes.

Conclusion for Gordon. Of the episodes that Gordon perceived to have positive influences, his common themes were positive family and school environments. Two quotes relative to Gordon's themes were: "That's the only time that they showed a family" and "I saw myself able to learn in that classroom."

Of the episodes that Gordon perceived to have negative influences, his common themes were stereotypes of African-Americans, such as "jokes about Black leaders, politicians, or Black activists" and "Black people are portrayed as hoodlums."

Subquestion III: What Changes in Perceptions Took Place When Interviewees Considered What Other Ethnic Audiences May Think About African-Americans as a Result of the Episodes' Images?

As discussed in Chapter III, I posed five major questions to the interviewees. Three of those questions were as follows:

- Would you feel differently about yourself and/or this episode if you viewed the episode with a White-American audience versus an African-American audience?

- What would you think about yourself and/or this episode if you knew that the world's populace were viewing it?

- What do you think other ethnic people would learn from this episode?

Occasionally, during the course of the interview, when I posed the three questions, the interviewees reversed their earlier statements that were made prior to the three questions. However, most interviewees' final perceptions of the episodes did not change. Sometimes the subsequent statements and the final perceptions did not correlate.

Moreover, oftentimes, when the interviewees were asked to express their feelings and thoughts about a particular episode, they did not articulate *their* feelings and thoughts. Instead, the interviewees expressed assumptions about White-Americans' and/or other ethnic peoples' feelings and thoughts pertaining to a particular episode.

For example, in Show II, Episode 1, I asked Keri, "Would you feel differently about yourself and this episode if you viewed the episode with a White-American audience?" Keri answered, "More than likely, a White-American audience would laugh and make certain comments. I'm sure they would say, 'Oh, I expected that from them.'"

It was interesting that the aforementioned statement was given by Keri, although I did not elicit the statement.

Tables 4 through 13 present the interviewees' data relative to Subquestion III. There is one table per interviewee. Because of time constraints pertaining to each episode, I made a judgment not to ask all of the three questions per episode or not to ask any of the three questions relative to particular episodes. Therefore, some questions, shows, and episodes are not shown per interviewee.

I made the following observations relative to Subquestion III:

• After considering how he would feel about the episodes, Leroy made no changes in his perceptions of what other ethnic audiences may think about African-Americans as a result of the images of these particular episodes (see Table 4).

• After considering what she would think and feel about herself relative to the episodes, Keri made two changes in her perceptions of what other ethnic audiences may think about African-Americans as a result of the images of these particular episodes (see Table 5).

- After considering what he would think and feel about himself relative to the episodes, John made one change in his perceptions of what other ethnic audiences may think about African-Americans as a result of the images of these particular episodes (see Table 6).

- After considering what he would think and feel about himself relative to the episodes, Ahmed made no changes in his perceptions of what other ethnic audiences may think about African-Americans as a result of the images of these particular episodes (see Table 7).

- After considering what she would think and feel about herself relative to the episodes, Elizabeth made one change in her perceptions of what other ethnic audiences may think about African-Americans as a result of the images of these particular episodes (see Table 8).

- After considering what she would think and feel about herself relative to the episodes, Barbara made no changes in her perceptions of what other ethnic audiences may think about African-Americans as a result of the images of these particular episodes (see Table 9).

- After considering what she would think and feel about herself relative to the episodes, Lisa made one change in her perceptions of what other ethnic audiences may think about African-Americans as a result of the images of these particular episodes (see Table 10).

- After considering what she would think and feel about herself relative to the episodes, Thelma made one change in her perceptions of what other ethnic audiences may think about African-Americans as a result of the images of these particular episodes (see Table 11).

• After considering what he would think and feel about himself relative to the episodes, David made one change in his perceptions of what other ethnic audiences may think about African-Americans as a result of the images of these particular episodes (see Table 12).

• After considering what he would think and feel about himself relative to the episodes, Gordon made one change in his perceptions of what other ethnic audiences may think about African-Americans as a result of the images of these particular episodes (see Table 13).

Summary of Interviewees' Data for Subquestion III. Three of the ten interviewees made no changes in their perceptions after considering what other ethnic audiences may think about African-Americans as a result of the images of particular episodes.

Six of the ten interviewees made one change in their perceptions after considering what other ethnic audiences may think about African-Americans as a result of the images of particular episodes.

One of the ten interviewees made two changes in her perceptions after considering what other ethnic audiences may think about African-Americans as a result of the images of particular episodes.

Conclusion for Subquestion III. It would be important research to query why the interviewees perceived some images to be positive; that is, why the images were perceived to be "funny" and/or "just a joke". Yet, the fact is that *all* of the episodes were couched in comedy. It would be worthwhile to

Table 4
Interviewee Response to Subquestion III: Leroy

SHOW/ Episode	Original Response	Subsequent Question	Subsequent Statement	Response Change
SHOW I Episode 2	+	Would you feel differently about yourself and/or this episode if you viewed this episode with a White-American audience versus an African-American audience?	White people might see it in a different aspect than I do. I see it as just humor. They might consider it to be a stereotype. But it doesn't affect me. If I were watching it with them, I would be on the defensive. They can't relate to it like I can. They are laughing at, not with, them (Black-Americans).	None
SHOW II Episode 3	+	Would you feel differently about yourself and/or this episode if you viewed this episode with a White-American audience versus an African-American audience?	If I was in a room full of White people, I don't think they would laugh because, unless they grew up with Black people, they can't relate to that.	None
SHOW III Episode 4	−	Would you feel differently about yourself and/or this episode if you viewed this episode with a White-American audience versus an African-American audience?	If a White audience was here, it would touch me. That's probably the way they see Black women or Black people as a whole. I guess the White people would feel superior.	None

+   =   Positive
−   =   Negative
+/− =   Positive/Negative (Hybrid)

Table 5

Interviewee Response to Subquestion III: Keri

SHOW/ Episode	Original Response	Subsequent Question	Subsequent Statement	Response Change
SHOW I Episode 1	+	What do you think other ethnic people would learn from this episode?	You know, we can relate to that. Other people out of our nationality might not be able to relate to that. They might laugh at the jokes and laugh at the rhythm that we have, but they probably won't get the same understanding as an African-American would. ... I believe it would be more negative because they would see Reverend Jackson as a comedian instead of a politician.	—
SHOW I Episode 2	+/−	What would you think about yourself and/or this episode if you knew that the world's populace were viewing it?	I would feel uncomfortable because they (Black people) are not all like that. Are they (the creatures of the show) trying to prove a point or are they trying to come up with a joke?	—
SHOW II Episode 1	−	Would you feel differently about yourself and/or this episode if you viewed this episode with a White-American audience versus an African-American audience?	More than likely, a White-American audience would laugh and make certain comments. I'm sure they would say, "Oh, I expected that from them."	None

Continued, next page

Table 5 – continued

SHOW/ Episode	Original Response	Subsequent Question	Subsequent Statement	Response Change
SHOW II Episode 4	+	What would you think about yourself and/or this episode if you knew that the world's populace were viewing it?	I believe that if White people don't know who this character is portraying, they would get a negative view; but if the viewers are aware of the character he is portraying, they might get a positive view.	None
SHOW II Episode 6	+	1. Would you feel differently about yourself and/or this episode if you viewed this episode with a White-American audience versus an African-American audience?	I wouldn't perceive it, but it would be perceived as being more negative than positive. ... I like the family image. ... The only thing is that I feel as if we were being portrayed as being ass backwards ... but, I believe the pros outweigh the cons.	None
		2. What would you think about yourself and/or this episode if you knew that the world's populace were viewing it?		
SHOW III Episode 3	+/–	What would you think about yourself and/or this episode if you knew that the world's populace were viewing it?	I would think that it would make me think less of myself, but I don't think that imagery is stereotypical of Black males.	None

Continued, next page

Table 5 – continued

SHOW/ Episode	Original Response	Subsequent Question	Subsequent Statement	Response Change
SHOW IV Episode 5	+	What would you think about yourself and/or this episode if you knew that the world's populace were viewing it?	I believe I would be comfortable because the lady had a job. Once the man came out of prison, he was on the right track. He was trying to do the right thing, but the only thing is she was trying to change him and he wouldn't allow her to change him. I think anyone can relate to that type of situation.	None

+ = Positive − = Negative +/− = Positive/Negative (Hybrid)

Table 6

Interviewee Response to Subquestion III: John

SHOW/ Episode	Original Response	Subsequent Question	Subsequent Statement	Response Change
SHOW I Episode 2	–	What would you think about yourself and/or this episode if you knew that the world's populace were viewing it?	If you had a majority of mixed races looking at this, they would sort of perceive, even though it's funny, they would still perceive a negative image about Black people.	None
SHOW I Episode 3	+	What would you think about yourself and/or this episode if you knew that the world's populace were viewing it?	If showed that he (Black male character) was positive throughout the whole episode; really, the White character showed how ignorant he was. ... The White character showed how distorted their views are about a lot of things.	None
SHOW I Episode 5	+/–	What would you think about yourself and/or this episode if you knew that the world's populace were viewing it?	I would feel happy within myself because when a person looks at that and comes up to me and thinks that I was living that way, I'd show them that I'm not. That isn't the image that I portray. ...In this country, that is, the picture of the average bum ... is the Black American male.	–

Continued, next page

Table 6 – continued

SHOW/ Episode	Original Response	Subsequent Question	Subsequent Statement	Response Change
SHOW II Episode 4	–	What would you think about yourself and/or this episode if you knew that the world's populace were viewing it?	It would make us look uncreative. This was like a Sambo type of imagery.	None
SHOW II Episode 6	+	What would you think about yourself and/or this episode if you knew that the world's populace were viewing it?	If somebody is able to relate that to us, any negative thoughts towards us, I would like to speak to them. I would like to see how they can relate that to us because that was pure comedy. I don't think anybody would relate that to Black-Americans. ... It is funny.	None
SHOW III Episode 1	–	What do you think other ethnic people would learn from this episode?	They would probably think that it is a good episode and say, "Yes, that's the way we want them to act."	None
SHOW III Episode 3	–	What would you think about yourself and/or this episode if you knew that the world's populace were viewing it?	I would feel positive because I don't think people would think that all Africans are gay or football players.	None

Continued, next page

Table 6 – continued

SHOW/ Episode	Original Response	Subsequent Question	Subsequent Statement	Response Change
SHOW IV Episode 1	−	1. Would you feel differently about yourself and/or this episode if you viewed this episode with a White-American audience versus an African-American audience? 2. What would you think about yourself and/or this episode if you knew that the world's populace were viewing it?	I would feel disturbed because they (White people) would think that all Black people are just money hungry. The sergeant speaks for himself. ...The people of the world would probably love him. He's your ideal Black man. But the bum only wants money so he can buy more booze or some drugs.	None
SHOW IV Episode 4	+	What would you think about yourself and/or this episode if you knew that the world's populace were viewing it?	I really wouldn't be concerned about this episode being shown to other people because there is nothing there. I mean, he isn't cursing; that's a positive image and everybody can see it.	None
SHOW IV Episode 5	+	Would you feel differently about yourself and/or this episode if you viewed this episode with a White-American audience versus an African-American audience?	I would feel kind of good because he's strong. His character represents strength to me. So, I would feel kind of comfortable in the room with other people.	None

= = Positive   − = Negative   +/− = Positive/Negative (Hybrid)

+ = Positive

Table 7
Interviewee Response to Subquestion III: Ahmed

SHOW/ Episode	Original Response	Subsequent Question	Subsequent Statement	Response Change
SHOW I Episode 1	+/−	What would you think about yourself and/or this episode if you knew that the world's populace were viewing it?	To the African-American community, I think that it could be something that could be humorous and they might enjoy it. But other groups of people, being that the way Mr. Jackson is already perceived in the press, would just add something more negative about him. So, that's the conflict that I have about skits like that.	None
SHOW I Episode 3	−	What would you think about yourself and/or this episode if you knew that the world's populace were viewing it?	I think that it loses something after it leaves our community, and I think that it tends to add to the stereotypes. I have hard times because people have their own views with shows like this that tend to make my life more complicated at times.	None
SHOW I Episode 5	−	What would you think about yourself and/or this episode if you knew that the world's populace were viewing it?	If I was watching this with someone else, who was outside my race, it wouldn't be something that I could feel proud of; it would make me feel uncomfortable.	None

Continued, next page

Table 7 – continued

SHOW/ Episode	Original Response	Subsequent Question	Subsequent Statement	Response Change
SHOW II Episode 1	+/-	Would you feel differently about yourself and/or this episode if you viewed this episode with a White-American audience versus an African-American audience?	I think that it would still be funny, because the skit as a whole is funny. ... If it was a predominately White audience, I don't think it's a character that they would take seriously.	None
SHOW II Episode 3	–	What would you think about yourself and/or this episode if you knew that the world's populace were viewing it?	It complicates the issue that much more ... if this is the only thing that's being sent out about us and that's what people as a whole feel about us. ... Sometimes, I've noticed that people who come from parts of the Caribbean and Africa have an attitude that we (Black-Americans) don't want anything. That we are helpless, that we identify with our helplessness and then try to scrape together anything that we can get versus looking for means of self-empowerment and liberation. So for a worldwide scope, it really hurts us negatively because we can't send enough role models out to give the true side of the picture.	None

Table 7 – continued

SHOW/ Episode	Original Response	Subsequent Question	Subsequent Statement	Response Change
SHOW III Episode 2	–	What would you think about yourself and/or this episode if you knew that the world's populace were viewing it?	If I was watching this with a non-African-American audience, they would find it to be funny. ... These kinds of programs are giving a negative image about ourselves. If we hold them in that kind of low esteem, how can we expect other people to respect our heroes as well as us as a whole?	None
SHOW IV Episode 4	–	What do you think other ethnic people would learn from these episodes?	The last step is, how do you get people who are on the international scale, if these images are sent out about us .... how do you say to those people, "We are people who are proud, who know our history, who have respect for ourselves?	None

+ = Positive
– = Negative
+/– = Positive/Negative (Hybrid)

Table 8

Interviewee Response to Subquestion III: Elizabeth

SHOW/ Episode	Original Response	Subsequent Question	Subsequent Statement	Response Change
SHOW II Episode 3	+/–	Would you feel differently about yourself and/or this episode if you viewed this episode with a White-American audience versus an African-American audience?	I probably would be more reserved if I was with a White audience, but this culture (Black) is familiar to me. That's why I take it light-spirited. Than, again, I might not really laugh if it was a White audience. ... I would probably take it to be negative because for all intents and purposes, they (White people) wouldn't be able to appreciate the culture.	–
SHOW II Episode 4	+	Would you feel differently about yourself and/or this episode if you viewed this episode with a White-American audience versus an African-American audience?	I probably wouldn't feel any differently if I was seated with another ethnic audience. I just see this as a spoof. I think it's light and cute.	None
SHOW III Episode 2	–	What would you think about yourself and/or this episode if you knew that the world's populace were viewing it?	I would not feel good because, unfortunately, I mean that's how we are always portrayed.	None

Continued, next page

Table 8 – continued

SHOW/ Episode	Original Response	Subsequent Question	Subsequent Statement	Response Change
SHOW III Episode 3	–	What would you think about yourself and/or this episode if you knew that the world's populace were viewing it?	I would feel uncomfortable because that is not a true representation of Black men who may be homosexual.	None

```
+   =   Positive
–   =   Negative
+/– =   Positive/Negative (Hybrid)
```

Table 9

Interviewee Response to Subquestion III: Barbara

SHOW/ Episode	Original Response	Subsequent Question	Subsequent Statement	Response Change
SHOW I Episode 1	+	Would you feel differently about yourself and/or this episode if you viewed this episode with a White-American audience versus an African-American audience?	Since I know the White audience would like Bob Hope, it'll probably be positive with the White group.	None
SHOW I Episode 5	–	What would you think about yourself and/or this episode if you knew that the world's populace were viewing it?	Maybe they (White people) should try to help the people.... try to do something about the poverty. ... They would have to see it as a stereotype. If they don't, then something is wrong with them.	None
SHOW II Episode 3	–	What would you think about yourself and/or this episode if you knew that the world's populace were viewing it?	I would hope it would be a negative stereotype. If this is shown in Europe, I hope they wouldn't think that everybody that's in the projects hang their clothes on the line and act like gossiping little hens.	None

Continued, next page

Table 9 – continued

SHOW/ Episode	Original Response	Subsequent Question	Subsequent Statement	Response Change
SHOW III Episode 1	–	What would you think about yourself and/or this episode if you knew that the world's populace were viewing it?	It would be a concern because, then, they (the world's people) would take them (Black people) for being stupid and not knowledgeable.	None
SHOW III Episode 2	+	What would you think about yourself and/or this episode if you knew that the world's populace were viewing it?	They would think that would be funny.	None
SHOW III Episode 3	+	Would you feel differently about yourself and/or this episode if you viewed this episode with a White-American audience versus an African-American audience?	I'd feel the same way.	None
SHOW III Episode 4	+/–	Would you feel differently about yourself and/or this episode if you viewed this episode with a White-American audience versus an African-American audience?	No, my opinion stands firm.	None

Continued, next page

Table 9 – continued

SHOW/ Episode	Original Response	Subsequent Question	Subsequent Statement	Response Change
SHOW IV Episode 1	+/–	Would you feel differently about yourself and/or this episode if you viewed this episode with a White-American audience versus an African-American audience?	Well, that one might make me feel a little uneasy, but I would still have my same opinion. I would hope that they would not see that as every Black person trying to join the army to get off the streets.	None

+   =   Positive
–   =   Negative
+/–   =   Positive/Negative (Hybrid)

Table 10
Interviewee Response to Subquestion III: Lisa

SHOW/ Episode	Original Response	Subsequent Question	Subsequent Statement	Response Change
SHOW I Episode 4	–	Would you feel differently about yourself and/or this episode if you viewed this episode with a White-American audience versus an African-American audience?	If I viewed this with a White audience, I would have the same feeling.	None
SHOW I Episode 5	+	What would you think about yourself and/or this episode if you knew that the world's populace were viewing it?	If other people in the world felt that a majority of Black people were in that situation, it would probably bother me. But it wouldn't make any difference if people just viewed it as just a funny skit.	None
SHOW II Episode 1	+	What would you think about yourself and/or this episode if you knew that the world's populace were viewing it?	I feel he was trying to bring across a message; I don't think he was saying anything negative about African-Americans.	None
SHOW II Episode 4	+	Would you feel differently about yourself and/or this episode if you viewed this episode with a White-American audience versus an African-American audience?	They (White people) could perceive this man as one who stands around making noises. It so, they (White people) really don't understand what was going on.	None

Continued, next page

Table 10 – continued

SHOW/ Episode	Original Response	Subsequent Question	Subsequent Statement	Response Change
SHOW II Episode 6	+	Would you feel differently about yourself and/or this episode if you viewed this episode with a White-American audience versus an African-American audience?	I don't know how anybody else in the world probably views it because I don't know how they would see it. Personally, I think I would still feel that it was positive.	None
SHOW III Episode 2	–	What do you think other ethnic people would learn from this episode?	They (White people) may perceive it to be negative because they may get it in their heads that all Black-Americans don't stick to this and they (Black-Americans) don't stick to that.	None
SHOW III Episode 3	+	1. Would you feel differently about yourself and/or this episode if you viewed this episode with a White-American audience versus an African-American audience?	I wouldn't be bothered; just, in general, I would not be bothered. I think he (the actor) was trying to exaggerate on a stereotype to see the silliness in it. ... I hope it would make them (White people) think positively, not negatively.	None
		2. What do you think other ethnic people would learn from this episode?		

Continued, next page

Table 10 – continued

SHOW/ Episode	Original Response	Subsequent Question	Subsequent Statement	Response Change
SHOW III Episode 4	–	What do you think other ethnic people would learn from this episode?	A lot of closed-minded people probably would think that's how they (Black people) always are. But if you look at it with an open mind, you can see that they are exaggerating a point.	None
SHOW IV Episode 1	+	What would you think about yourself and/or this episode if you knew that the world's populace were viewing it?	I feel good about myself. I would still feel the same way if I knew other people in the world were viewing this episode.	None
SHOW IV Episode 4	+/–	1. Would you feel differently about yourself and/or this episode if you viewed this episode with a White-American audience versus an African-American audience?	I don't know if I would feel so good because I would think they (White audience) see Black people putting down other Black people. ... White people might feel: Why should they change the way they think and feel about us if we don't change ourselves?	–
		2. What would you think about yourself and/or this episode if you knew that the world's populace were viewing it?	I probably wouldn't feel so good about the world's audiences viewing this episode.	

Continued, next page

Table 10 – continued

SHOW/ Episode	Original Response	Subsequent Question	Subsequent Statement	Response Change
SHOW IV Episode 5	+	What do you think other ethnic people would learn from this episode?	If other people in the world were viewing it with a closed mind, they probably would think that he was lazy, didn't want to work. But if they were viewing it with an open mind, they would see that he's not lazy. It's just that he wanted to work for himself.	None

+   =   Positive
–   =   Negative
+/– =   Positive/Negative (Hybrid)

Table 11

Interviewee Response to Subquestion III: Thelma

SHOW/ Episode	Original Response	Subsequent Question	Subsequent Statement	Response Change
SHOW I Episode 2	+/–	What would you think about yourself and/or this episode if you knew that the world's populace were viewing it?	Not too good.	–
SHOW I Episode 4	–	What do you think other ethnic people would learn from this episode?	They would probably laugh. Other people would probably believe this if they are not around Black people enough to know that is not how we act.	None
SHOW I Episode 5	+/–	Would you feel differently about yourself and/or this episode if you viewed this episode with a White-American audience versus an African-American audience?	No, I'd feel the same way.	None
SHOW II Episode 1	–	What would you think about yourself and/or this episode if you knew that the world's populace were viewing it?	They (other ethnic people) would try to keep a Black person in jail if they saw this type of thing.	None

Continued, next page

Table 11 – continued

SHOW/ Episode	Original Response	Subsequent Question	Subsequent Statement	Response Change
SHOW II Episode 2	+	Would you feel differently about yourself and/or this episode if you viewed this episode with a White-American audience versus an African-American audience?	My feelings would be the same.	None
SHOW II Episode 3	–	What would you think about yourself and/or this episode if you knew that the world's populace were viewing it?	When you look at a Black person, you feel that all of them are like that and that is not true.	None
SHOW II Episode 4	+	Would you feel differently about yourself and/or this episode if you viewed this episode with a White-American audience versus an African-American audience?	Yes, I would feel that same way if I were seated with a White-American audience while viewing this episode.	None
SHOW II Episode 6	+	Would you feel differently about yourself and/or this episode if you viewed this episode with a White-American audience versus an African-American audience?	I would feel the same.	None

Continued, next page

Table 11 -- continued

SHOW/ Episode	Original Response	Subsequent Question	Subsequent Statement	Response Change
SHOW III Episode 1	-	What do you think other ethnic people would learn from this episode?	They (other ethnic people) would probably look at it the same way that I'm looking at it.	None
SHOW III Episode 2	+/-	Would you feel differently about yourself and/or this episode if you viewed this episode with a White-American audience versus an African-American audience?	It's my opinion whether I'm sitting there with a White audience or an Hispanic audience. It's always going to be my opinion.	None
SHOW III Episode 3	+	Would you feel differently about yourself and/or this episode if you viewed this episode with a White-American audience versus an African-American audience?	Because, again, it's my opinion ...a White-American audience would look at it as, "Oh, why are they letting a homosexual teach the class?" The Whites would probably think that all Black people are homosexuals because they are dancing. That's just their (Black people) way of showing how happy they were to win.	None
SHOW III Episode 4	-	What do you think other ethnic people would learn from this episode?	They (other people) would look at the show and say, "I suppose that's how all Blacks act," and they would not want to come around us.	None

Continued, next page

Table 11 – continued

SHOW/ Episode	Original Response	Subsequent Question	Subsequent Statement	Response Change
SHOW IV Episode 1	+/–	Would you feel differently about yourself and/or this episode if you viewed this episode with a White-American audience versus an African-American audience?	It's my opinion that he didn't treat the bum badly. I would not feel differently if White-Americans were watching this episode.	None
SHOW IV Episode 2	+/–	Would you feel differently about yourself and/or this episode if you viewed this episode with a White-American audience versus an African-American audience?	Maybe, maybe not. I wouldn't know. They (White-Americans) wouldn't probably look at it the way I'm looking at it. They would probably look at it differently.	None
SHOW IV Episode 5	+/–	Would you feel differently about yourself and/or this episode if you viewed this episode with a White-American audience versus an African-American audience?	Yes, I would feel the same.	None

+   =   Positive
–   =   Negative
+/– =   Positive/Negative (Hybrid)

Table 12

Interviewee Response to Subquestion III: David

SHOW/ Episode	Original Response	Subsequent Question	Subsequent Statement	Response Change
SHOW I Episode 1	+	Would you feel differently about yourself and/or this episode if you viewed this episode with a White-American audience versus an African-American audience?	I still think it's positive.	None
SHOW I Episode 2	–	What would you think about yourself and/or this episode if you knew that the world's populace were viewing it?	They (other ethnic people) probably would get another stereotype about us, like some people have already done showing us with big lips, dancing and shuffling! So this would probably be another one for their collection.	None
SHOW I Episode 4	+/–	Would you feel differently about yourself and/or this episode if you viewed this episode with a White-American audience versus an African-American audience?	See that changes everything. So many of them (White people) I know, because I went to Penn State. ... Many of them were from small towns and the only image of Blacks, that they saw, was on television. They see us as illiterate and uneducated. So my thinking would probably be a little different.	–

Continued, next page

Table 12 – continued

SHOW/ Episode	Original Response	Subsequent Question	Subsequent Statement	Response Change
SHOW II Episode 1	+	Would you feel differently about yourself and/or this episode if you viewed this episode with a White-American audience versus an African-American audience?	This shows what really happens to the Black man in America.	None
SHOW II Episode 2	+	Would you feel differently about yourself and/or this episode if you viewed this episode with a White-American audience versus an African-American audience?	This goes beyond the color line. It happens to Blacks, Whites, Latinos, and Asians. It doesn't matter.	None
SHOW II Episode 3	+/–	Would you feel differently about yourself and/or this episode if you viewed this episode with a White-American audience versus an African-American audience?	No, they (White-Americans) would probably see it as being a Black female. But I, being a Black man, would see this as being a universal character.	None
SHOW II Episode 4	+	What would you think about yourself and/or this episode if you knew that the world's populace were viewing it?	I think so, yes. Yes, because I would think they would see it as a comedic piece.	None

Continued, next page

Table 12 -- continued

SHOW/ Episode	Original Response	Subsequent Question	Subsequent Statement	Response Change
SHOW III Episode 1	--	What would you think about yourself and/or this episode if you knew that the world's populace were viewing it?	Not good because, unfortunately, this is part of the new way of dealing with things. Black senators, people in politics become ultra-conservative, become Republican, think White, act White or even marry White so it will improve their cause.	None
SHOW III Episode 2	--	Would you feel differently about yourself and/or this episode if you viewed this episode with a White-American audience versus an African-American audience?	When White people see this, it's like, that's how they are, you know, the big mammy role. They always have fried eggs, bacon, ham, and all of this other stuff.	None
SHOW III Episode 3	--	What would you think about yourself and/or this episode if you knew that the world's populace were viewing it?	Definitely, I would be disturbed because T. V. is probably the most powerful medium known to man.	None
SHOW III Episode 4	--	What would you think about yourself and/or this episode if you knew that the world's populace were viewing it?	You know that a wider audience is seeing this and they are going with the stereotypes because visual image is probably the most effective image known.	None

Continued, next page

Table 12 – continued

SHOW/ Episode	Original Response	Subsequent Question	Subsequent Statement	Response Change
SHOW III Episode 5	–	Would you feel differently about yourself and/or this episode if you viewed this episode with a White-American audience versus an African-American audience?	Yes, this one episode goes beyond the color line.	None
SHOW IV Episode 4	–	What would you think about yourself and/or this episode if you knew that the world's populace were viewing it?	It would bother me because they (other ethnic people) would get an unfair assessment of the Black man.	None
SHOW IV Episode 5	+/–	1. Would you feel differently about yourself and/or this episode if you viewed this episode with a White-American audience versus an African-American audience?	It would give them (other ethnic people) something else to build up their library of stereotypes about Black men. ... White people would probably laugh because the male character is a funny individual and he plays off other people.	None
		2. What would you think about yourself and/or this episode if you knew that the world's populace were viewing it?		

+   =   Positive
–   =   Negative
+/– =   Positive/Negative (Hybrid)

Table 13

Interviewee Response to Subquestion III: Gordon

SHOW/ Episode	Original Response	Subsequent Question	Subsequent Statement	Response Change
SHOW I Episode 2	–	Would you feel differently about yourself and/or this episode if you viewed this episode with a White-American audience versus an African-American audience?	I'd feel bad. It puts you in the corner of a room, and it doesn't make you feel good. It really doesn't.	None
SHOW II Episode 1	+/–	1. Would you feel differently about yourself and/or this episode if you viewed this episode with a White-American audience versus an African-American audience?	I see the message in that show, whereas a lot of people won't see the message because they just don't take time to understand that there are other people in the world besides them who have problems. ... I wish a lot of people would see this so that they would know what's going on in a Black community. If you don't understand what's happening in the Black community, you'll just see a clown joking around and having a negative image of Black people.	None
		2. What would you think about yourself and/or this episode if you knew that the world's populace were viewing it?		

Continued, next page

Table 13 – continued

SHOW/ Episode	Original Response	Subsequent Question	Subsequent Statement	Response Change
SHOW II Episode 6	+	Would you feel differently about yourself and/or this episode if you viewed this episode with a White-American audience versus an African-American audience?	I'd feel uncomfortable viewing this with a White audience because it's Blacks being portrayed as having that ass basically right there. I would feel uncomfortable.	–
SHOW III Episode 3	+/–	What would you think about yourself and/or this episode if you knew that the world's populace were viewing it?	I wouldn't like it because it portrays dancers, especially African-American dancers, as homosexuals and a lot of them aren't. As far as the football players, there's nothing racial or degrading about that to me. The spiking of the football, I've seen guys do that.	None

+   =   Positive
–   =   Negative
+/– =   Positive/Negative (Hybrid)

inquire why, in some instances, the interviewees did not perceive a particular episode to have stereotypes until I posed one of the aforementioned three questions under Question 1, Subquestion III. Finally, the interviewees' statements, noted in Tables 4-13, suggest that it would be worthwhile to investigate why (when the audience is White or the world's other ethnic people) some of the African-American young adults felt uncomfortable about the television images of African-Americans. Conversely, they felt comfortable about the African-American images, while seated with an African-American audience. This is another significant factor to be included in further research.

This concludes the data analysis for Question 2.

REVIEW OF HYBRID EPISODES

The interviewees communicated many mixed responses; that is, they perceived many episodes to have positive *and* negative influences. These episodes are hybrids.

Leroy was the only interviewee who did not perceive any episodes to be hybrids. The interviewees' responses relative to some of the hybrid episodes are as follow.

* **Keri**

Show III, Episode 1: I would expect a Harvard graduate to be a little more self-contained, able to handle themselves. They were extremely foolish. . . . The way this is portrayed, it was wrong. The positive is that you can go to Harvard and you will still make it.

Show I, Episode 5: It makes you feel kind of good, but it also makes you feel sad in the sense that you have people out there who are living like that. . . . Whenever you deal with poverty like that, it's always negative; but it's comedy and it's hard to be judgmental when it's comedy like that. It was negative in the sense that they were showing a poor person; but in spite of everything, I guess you have to say, it's kind of positive. No matter what, the person is surviving, and that's the bottom line.

- **Ahmed**

Show I, Episode 1: To the African-American community, I think that it could be something that could be humorous and they might enjoy it. But other groups of people, being the way Reverend Jackson is already perceived in the press, would add to something more negative about him. So, that's the conflict that I run together with skits like that on a whole.

- **Elizabeth**

Show II, Episode 3: I guess you can view it as sort of bringing to light some of the problems that we have. Then, again, on the flip side, it's negative because some people don't have a more expansive perception . . . although I may chuckle. Then, again, it's sad.

- **Barbara**

Show III, Episode 4: As the parent pushing the little girl to become a star or try to become this overnight success, I see myself a little bit in that because I think every little girl has a dream of becoming either a model or an actress. . . . The mother should be ashamed of herself for trying to get this girl and actually making this man watch her daughter and making the whole production a mess. As far as me seeing myself in it, it's a little like being a "star," but then it turns negative because it goes to the extreme.

- **Lisa**

Show IV, Episode 4: It's kind of sad because a lot of rappers refer to women as "hoes" and I think that's kind of negative. . . . It made me think about myself in a positive way because I know he's just making a generalization and that he's just going on basically his experiences which might not have been broad.

- **Thelma**

Show I, Episode 2: This didn't really affect me. It's funny, so it's not as bad as Episode 1. . . . They could be taken positive because most Black people make it in the world by being funny. But then again, if there's somebody White watching it, they'll say, "A Black person is only supposed to be taken as a joke." So it's not really positive.

- **David**

Show IV, Episode 1: In reference to the Army officer, it shows that we can achieve rank. That was positive. But then, on the other hand, you have the homeless guy. That shows the total opposite, the negative aspect – uneducated, you know, smelly, and all that.

- **Gordon**

Show II, Episode 1: You'd look and say it's negative because it portrays an ex-convict who can't find a job and has a sour look on life. But then you look at it positively and say, "All right, it's true. Black people who come out of jail, especially Black men who come out of jail, can't find jobs anywhere." Within that skit, he was denied an education and that White establishment won't let him move up. You're looking at a Black man who's trying to be something with his life, but he can't.

Finally, as the reader examines the "Researcher's Data Matrix" (see Table 3) horizontally, the reader can see this data.

- **Show I, Episode 1**

Six interviewees perceived this episode to have a positive influence, three interviewees perceived this episode to have a negative influence, and one interviewee perceived this episode to have a hybrid influence.

- **Show I, Episode 2**

One interviewee perceived this episode to have a positive influence, eight interviewees perceived this episode to have a negative influence, and one interviewee perceived this episode to have a hybrid influence.

- **Show I, Episode 3**

One interviewee perceived this episode to have a positive influence, seven interviewees perceived this episode to have a negative influence, and two interviewees perceived this episode to have a hybrid influence.

- **Show I, Episode 4**
One interviewee perceived this episode to have a positive influence, seven interviewees perceived this episode to have a negative influence, and two interviewees perceived this episode to have a hybrid influence.

- **Show I, Episode 5**
One interviewee perceived this episode to have a positive influence, seven interviewees perceived this episode to have a negative influence, and two interviewees perceived this episode to have a hybrid influence.

- **Show II, Episode 1**
Four interviewees perceived this episode to have a positive influence, four interviewees perceived this episode to have a negative influence, and two interviewees perceived this episode to have a hybrid influence.

- **Show II, Episode 2**
Six interviewees perceived this episode to have a positive influence, and four interviewees perceived this episode to have a negative influence.

- **Show II, Episode 3**
One interviewee perceived this episode to have a positive influence, seven interviewees perceived this episode to have a negative influence, and two interviewees perceived this episode to have a hybrid influence.

- **Show II, Episode 4**
Five interviewees perceived this episode to have a positive influence, and five interviewees perceived this episode to have a negative influence.

- **Show II, Episode 5**
Not Black; therefore, not applicable.

- **Show II, Episode 6**
Five interviewees perceived this episode to have a positive influence, and five interviewees perceived this episode to have a negative influence.

- **Show III, Episode 1**
No interviewees perceived this episode to have a positive influence, eight interviewees perceived this episode to have a negative influence, and two interviewees perceived this episode to have a hybrid influence.

- **Show III, Episode 2**
Four interviewees perceived this episode to have a positive influence, five interviewees perceived this episode to have a negative influence, and one interviewee perceived this episode to have a hybrid influence.

- **Show III, Episode 3**
Two interviewees perceived this episode to have a positive influence, six interviewees perceived this episode to have a negative influence, and two interviewees perceived this episode to have a hybrid influence.

- **Show III, Episode 4**
No interviewees perceived this episode to have a positive influence, nine interviewees perceived this episode to have a negative influence, and one interviewee perceived this episode to have a hybrid influence.

- **Show III, Episode 5**
Four interviewees perceived this episode to have a positive influence, three interviewees perceived this episode to have a negative influence, and three interviewees perceived this episode to have a hybrid influence.

- **Show IV, Episode 1**
Two interviewees perceived this episode to have a positive influence, five interviewees perceived this episode to have a

negative influence, and three interviewees perceived this episode to have a hybrid influence.

• **Show IV, Episode 2**
No interviewees perceived this episode to have a positive influence, seven interviewees perceived this episode to have a negative influence, and three interviewees perceived this episode to have a hybrid influence.

• **Show IV, Episode 3**
Not Black; therefore, not applicable.

• **Show IV, Episode 4**
Two interviewees perceived this episode to have a positive influence, seven interviewees perceived this episode to have a negative influence, and one interviewee perceived this episode to have a hybrid influence.

• **Show IV, Episode 5**
Four interviewees perceived this episode to have a positive influence, four interviewees perceived this episode to have a negative influence, and two interviewees perceived this episode to have a hybrid influence.

SUMMARY

This chapter centered on the presentation and analysis of data from two major sources. First, the three judges analyzed the television images to determine if the substance of particular television programming was likely to have a positive or negative effect on young African-American adults. Although only a few program episodes were considered to have redeeming features, the three judges were in strong agreement that the selected program episodes may have a powerful negative influence.

Thirty hours of interviews with ten African-American adults revealed that the subjects differed in their perceptions of the possible influence of the television programming on their self-perceptions. Although differences in perceptions existed, only one respondent perceived all television episodes to have negative influences, except for the hybrids. Many of the episodes were viewed as having the potential for positive and negative influences. The judges perceived the television imageries to be negative. Yet the young African-Americans who were interviewed tended to see the same imagery as being positive. This difference in perception among different generations of African-Americans may be attributed to thoughts about humor and ridicule. Also, the limited life experiences of those being interviewed may influence their critical consciousness and thus contribute to the tendency to be more tolerant of the possible negative impact the images may have on their views of themselves.

Although the findings of this chapter may only be generalized to the judges and those interviewed, the results suggest that further research into the impact of television imagery on the way young African-American adults view themselves is a crucial problem for further research.

V

SUMMARY AND RECOMMENDATIONS

The purpose of this chapter is to summarize the present research. The problem, purpose, and design of the study are reviewed. Also, the major findings of the study are presented. Finally, five types of recommendations are advanced, including recommendations for further research, school reform, parents, television industry, and organizational development.

SUMMARY

The problem of this study is the possibility that television shows that portray African-American imageries may be influencing the self-perceptions of African-American young adults in negative ways. If so, the African-American young adults' self-perceptions may impede their personal and academic potential in American society.

The purpose of this study was to determine the possible influence of particular television imageries of African-Americans on the self-perceptions of selected young adult African-Americans, ages eighteen to twenty-five. Two major research questions guide the investigation:

- What specific aspects of self are addressed by particular television imageries of African-Americans?

- What possible influences do particular television imageries have on self-perceptions of selected young adult African-Americans?

The conceptual base for the two research questions was presented in the review of literature. The review centered on

(1) the influence of perception and human behavior and (2) the impact of television images on how individuals view themselves.

For part one, I justified why it is important to consider perceptions of individuals as a powerful force for determining how one thinks, feels, or acts. For part two, I explored the possibility that how young adult African-Americans view themselves may result, in part, from images of African-Americans they see on television. In the review of literature, I cited the exegeses of educators, behavioral and social scientists, journalists, historians who specialize in African-American history, and historians who specialize in television and movie history.

For the design of this exploratory study, I used a qualitative methodology to answer the two major research questions. I selected three African-American judges to participate in the study. The judges included one social psychologist, one anthropologist, and one psychiatrist who specialized in counseling young adults between the ages of seventeen to thirty. Each judge was asked to view four taped shows of a popular television series which features African-American characters. Each show consisted of five episodes. The judges were then asked to identify and analyze the positive and/or negative imageries that they thought may influence the self-concept of African-American young adults. Thus, the judges provided data to answer Question 1 ("What specific aspects of self are addressed by particular television imageries of African-Americans?").

Next, I conducted in-depth, individual interviews with ten young African-American adults. During the interview sessions, I presented to the interviewees the identical four shows that were viewed by the judges. Each session was audiotaped. Because each show contained five episodes, I stopped the show after each episode to orally question the interviewees about their perceptions of the episode.

I asked the same questions after each episode of each show. The questions were as follows:

- As an African-American, how does this episode make you *think* about yourself?

- As an African-American, how does this episode make you *feel* about yourself?

If time permitted, I added three more questions:

- Would you feel different about yourself and/or this episode if you viewed this episode with a White-American audience versus an African-American audience?

- What would you think about yourself and/or this episode if you knew that the world's populace were viewing it?

- What do you think other ethnic people would learn from this episode?

After the interview sessions were completed, I had the audiotapes transcribed. There were thirty hours of interviews and three hundred and thirty-seven transcribed pages. The data from the interviews were analyzed to answer Question 2 ("What possible influence do particular television imageries have on self-perceptions of selected young adult African-Americans?").

The Major Findings

In reviewing the major findings, first, I will reiterate the research question that guided the analyses from the judges: "What specific aspects of self are addressed by particular television imageries of African-Americans?" I divided the judges' responses into three categories for analysis. There were three subquestions which established the three categories. The first subquestion, with its major findings, was as follows: "What did the three judges determine were the positive or negative influences of the selected episodes on self?" All judges unitedly concurred that thirteen out of nineteen episodes were likely to have negative influences on self-concepts of young African-American adults. None of the judges concurred that any episodes were likely to have positive influences on self-concepts of young African-American adults. According to the judges' data, the episodes' reiterative messages posit that African-Americans' behaviors, attitudes, and values are negative. Therefore, it is reasonable to conclude that the episodes were viewed by the judges to have negative influences on the self.

The second subquestion relative to the judges and the major findings was as follows: "What does each judge consider to be the major likely influence on self?" The first judge, Dr. Kenneth B. Clark, stated explicitly that likely negative influences on self were "stereotypes of various sorts" and obstruct young adult African-Americans' possibilities to "emerge with a positive self-image from almost any one of the episodes."

Dr. Johnnetta B. Cole expressed that these "spoofs on African-American behavior can and do influence how African-Americans see themselves." Dr. Alvin F. Poussaint's exegesis about likely negative influences on self was how demeaning stereotypes can "deflate" the self.

The third subquestion with its major findings from the judges was as follows: "What likely influences were identified by all of the judges in the selected episodes?" All of the judges identified degrading stereotypes as the likely influences in the selected episodes. Some stereotypes that were identified by the judges as being attributable to African-Americans in the selected episodes were as follows:

- Dangerous and beast-like African-American men
- Dirty and repulsive African-American poor people
- African-Americans engaging in gross behavior, like spitting and fighting
- African-Americans disrespecting other African-Americans, such as men striking women, cursing, etc.

- Animalistic, sub-human African-American men
- African-American men who are buffoonish clowns
- African-American women as nosy, gossipy, hens
- African-Americans as welfare recipients who are dependent on welfare cheese
- African-American men being sexual studs
- Immoral, dirty, and incompetent African-Americans
- Undisciplined African-American children who strike African-American adults
- A hopeless African-American community which believes that unless you are White, you won't make it in society

I will restate the research question that directed the data from the ten interviewees. The question was: "What possible influences do particular television imageries have on self-perceptions of selected young African-Americans?" Again, as for the judges, I divided the interviewees' responses into three categories that were relevant to three subquestions. The first subquestion with its major findings was as follows: "Did the interviewees perceive the episodes to be positive or negative relating to their self-perceptions as African-Americans?" With the exception of one interviewee, all interviewees perceive some episodes to be positive. All interviewees perceived some episodes to be negative. With the exception of one interviewee, all interviewees perceived some episodes to be both positive and negative (hybrids).

The second subquestion regarding the ten interviewees and the major findings was as follows: "What were the positive and negative influences on the episodes as reported by the interviewees?" Two interviewees perceived more episodes to have positive than negative influences. Eight interviewees perceived more episodes to have negative influences. One interviewee perceived all episodes to have negative influences except for some hybrids, and nine interviewees perceived some episodes to be hybrids.

Additionally, none of the interviewees perceived all of the episodes to have positive influences. None of the interviewees perceived all of the episodes to have negative influences.

Some interviewees perceived episodes to have positive influences because the interviewees perceived the episodes to be humorous. Some interviewees perceived episodes to have negative influences because the interviewees perceived the episodes' characters to be stereotypical.

The third subquestion pertaining to the interviewees and the major findings was as follows: "What changes in perceptions took place when the interviewees considered what other ethnic audiences may think about African-Americans as a result of the episodes' images?" Three of the ten interviewees made no changes in their perceptions after considering what other ethnic audiences may think about African-Americans as a result of the images of the particular episodes. Six of the ten interviewees made one change to their perceptions after considering what other ethnic audiences may think about African-Americans as a result of the images of the particular episodes. One of the ten interviewees made two changes in her perceptions after considering what other ethnic audiences may think about African-Americans as a result of the images of the particular episodes.

What does it mean when all of the judges deem an episode to be negative and most of the interviewees deem an episode to be positive? (See Tables 2 and 3, respectively.) To answer this question, I consulted a psychologist who specializes in counseling adolescents and young adults. This psychologist is an African-American who is an Assistant Professor of Psychology in the Department of Psychiatry at Harvard Medical School in Boston, Massachusetts. Dr. Jessica Henderson Daniel (1992) offered the following answer:

> *While it is readily apparent that the two groups represent different generations of African-Americans, I believe that the difference can also be attributed to perceived importance of sociopolitical factors as well as to notions about humor and ridicule.*
>
> *In terms of the latter, the young people may feel that everybody and everything can be subject to 'humorous' presentations. The line between humor and ridicule may be fluid for some and nonexistent*

for others. Humor can be inclusive of the target, i.e., the individual may genuinely laugh at himself/herself or it can be emotionally devastating or demeaning. The feelings of the target may be relevant or irrelevant. Humor can be respectful or disrespectful. I would suspect that for many young people, except for when the humor is directed at them or at someone for whom they care, the above factors are not considered to the same degree as would be the case for the senior scholars. One explanation is that the differences between humor and ridicule are not recognized. . . . The scholars have all been active in the media and understand its power. They have also been exposed to racism and self-hatred in many forms, both within and outside the African-American community. They have lived with and seen the consequences. In contrast, the young people have more limited life experiences and are more 'here and now' oriented. One could say they represent different worlds of thought.

As Dr. Daniel unequivocally stated, young people, because of their youth, have "limited life experiences." So, understandably, African-American young adults might easily be influenced by the television imageries of African-Americans. This view was shared by the three judges. Furthermore, the results of the ten young adult African-American interviewees' data imply that television imageries of African-Americans may be influencing the self-perceptions of young adult African-Americans.

RECOMMENDATIONS

There are five types of implications that will be represented in this section. They are: Research, School Reform, Parents, Television Industry, and Organizational Development.

Research

This study was conducted with constraints; therefore, clearly, there are implications for further research. This study concentrated on television imageries influencing the self-perceptions of African-American young adults. Nevertheless, it is possible that television imageries are influencing the self-perceptions of other age groups, such as children and older adults. It is possible that television imageries are influencing the sexual attitudes of women, men, boys, and girls. It is possible that television imageries are influencing the racial perceptions of all people. It is possible that television imageries are influencing people's political, social, educational, and historical perspectives. Lastly, it is possible that television imageries are influencing behavior and/or actions of humans. All of the above should be investigated.

If I conducted another study on television imageries of African-American young adults' self-perceptions, I would explore the following questions:

- What happens to a person's image after she or he sees a television image? Does the person retain her or his image? (Kunjufu, 1984)

- Do African-American young adults recognize the differences between ridicule and humor? (Daniel, 1992)

- Are African-American young adults less discerning about television imageries while seated with an African-American audience versus a White-American audience?

- Is it bothersome to African-American young adults to view the African-American television imageries with White-Americans? If so, why is it so? If not, why not?

- Why do people see the same things differently?

Consequently, I believe that negative television imageries of African-Americans instruct African-Americans to hate themselves. Also, I believe that negative television imageries of African-Americans instruct other ethnic people to dislike African-Americans. Through further research, one might learn if television is a persuasive tool and a purveyor of racist messages.

School Reform

On February 25, 1992, the American Psychological Association issued a report stating that "American children spend more time watching television than they do in school; therefore, children should be taught 'critical viewing' skills" (Huston et al., 1992).

The following are some findings of the American Psychological Association about the effects of television on children (Huston et al., 1992):

- Advertisements to children are permeated with sugar-laden cereals, candy, fat-saturated chips, and fast foods.

- The rate of violence on prime time evening television is five to six incidents per hour; whereas the rate on Saturday morning programs is twenty to twenty-five acts per hour.

- Most ethnic minorities are virtually absent; when they do appear, they are often negatively stereotyped as criminals, dangerous characters, or victims of violence.

- Males are shown as major characters on the average of three times as often as females on prime time television.

- The predominant messages on television, which are highly stereotyped, can increase adolescents' sex-stereotyped beliefs and attitudes.

Because of this report, I suggest that educators construct curricula that will help to counter television's possible influence on elementary and high school children's self-perceptions and their perceptions of other people. Furthermore, there should be further research on whether the elementary and high school children's feelings, thoughts, and actions relative to themselves and others evolve from the television imageries that they view. Also, educators should implement strategies for teaching children to see that television is not necessarily a true medium for instruction. In other words, because children view many hours of television per day, educators should establish curricula that instruct children how to develop "critical viewing skills."

I suspect that children would be avid students in a classroom that focuses on how to analyze television imageries. Thereafter, possibly, the politics of racial and sexual prejudices and violence would be understood by children. What a wonderful accomplishment that would be for educators.

As referenced in Chapter I, educators can be the disconfirming agents relative to the propagandized television stereotypes of African-Americans and other people. Educators have a duty to rewrite textbooks that have grossly misinformed *all* Americans about the history of African-Americans and America's people.

Educators should devise a plan to train educators and to train potential teachers to counter the predominantly negative African-American television imageries and negative imageries of other people. Educators should self-examine *their* perceptions and whether they are conveying negative perceptions and beliefs to their students. If so, there should be counseling and behavioral training sessions for those teachers.

I, who is a parent and an African-American, have encountered teachers who conveyed racist ideas and prejudiced feelings to their students. I surmise that this might be a serious problem in many American schools. Additionally, I opine that some educators, because of their cultural and sexual prejudices, purposely communicate racist, confirming messages to their students. Also, I think that it is not the intention of some educators nor some of the people who comprise America's educational systems, to offer each student, regardless of culture, sex, or religion, a quintessential education. Because of that, the implication is some educators are not honest about their perceptions of their students. Even the educators' perceptions of others might stem from television imageries.

Parents

In addition to focusing on children's television viewing habits and the influential negative televised imageries, the American Psychological Association (APA) offered guidelines for parents. The APA stated that parents "are the first and perhaps most important teachers about how to use television" (Huston et al., 1992). The implications for parents are best stated by the APA report. Some recommendations for parents are the following (Huston, et al., 1992):

- Watch at least one episode of the programs the child watches to know how violent they are.

- When viewing television together, discuss the violence with the child. Talk about why the violence happened and how painful it is. Ask the child how conflict can be solved without violence.

- Encourage children to watch programs with characters that cooperate, help, and care for each other. These programs have been shown to influence children in a positive way.

- Ask children to compare what they see on the screen with people, places, and events they know firsthand, have read about, or studied in school.

- Encourage children to read newspapers, listen to the radio, talk to adults about their work, or meet people from different ethnic or social backgrounds.

- Tell children what is real and what is make believe on television. Explain how television uses stunt people, camera zooms, dream sequences, and animation to create fantasy.

- Tell children that the purpose of advertising is to sell products to as many viewers as possible.

- Teach the children a few facts about nutrition and then let him or her use them.

- Explain values your family holds about sex, alcohol, and drugs.

I believe that parents and children should exchange and verbalize feelings and thoughts pertaining to televised imageries. From this collaborative relationship, perhaps, children will acquire analytical skills relative to the television imageries that they view.

Television Industry

As a result of the major findings of this study, there are many implications for the television industry. The people and entities who maneuver the television industry are also responsible for most television imageries. Those people and entities are the television hegemonic strata. This strata should terminate their strategies of financing and creating negative depictions of African-Americans and other cultural people. The television hegemonic strata should terminate their practices of hiring, financing, and encouraging African-American writers, directors, producers, and actors to create negative imageries of African-Americans while excluding African-American writers, directors, producers, and actors who wish to create positive imageries of African-Americans. Two of many questions can be posed to members of the television hegemonic strata: Why do you create and finance negative television images of African-Americans? Who is benefiting from this?

Negative images of African-Americans propagandize misinformation about African-Americans. Another implication for the television industry is that negative images of other cultural people propagandize misinformation about those people also. By constructing "differences" based on color and sex, the "differences" become negative. Differences do not have to be negative. Television can be used as an educational tool to teach the world's populace to understand and appreciate people's cultural differences. Finally, an implication for the television industry is that television, as an educational tool, can educate the world's populace about human similarities which transcend cultural diversity.

Organizational Development

Throughout its history, the television industry has perpetuated stereotypical imageries of African-Americans. These stereotypical imageries reinforce biased encoding of messages relevant to so-called out-groups. An implication for organizational development specialists is to place emphasis on curricula that center on in-group and out-group behaviors. This curricula can clarify what is perceived in-group and out-group behaviors and, hopefully, the curricula can eliminate the myths and labels relative to in-groups and out-groups.

Because the television industry has continually reinforced and sustained stereotypes of African-Americans, there is no reason to believe that the television hegemonic strata is willing to create positive changes relative to African-American television imageries. Consequently, organizational development specialists should develop strategies to make the television industry change its mission.

Organizational development impacts individuals and groups that embody organizations. According to Pfeiffer and Ballew (1991), "a change in an organizational system occurs as a response to disturbances from within or outside the organizations. . . . An internal or external stimulus leads to a response."

Havelock (1973) constructed four primary modes for facilitating organizational change. I will list and apply each primary mode to the television industry, which is an organization. The four primary modes are as follows:

The Change Agent as Catalyzer. Apparently, it is in the interests of the television hegemonic strata to not change the negative imageries of African-Americans. Necessarily, an external stimulus/external change agent must perform as the catalyzer. The catalyzers/external change agents are the targets of the negative television imageries: the television viewers. Educators, as sponsors, can teach viewers to be critical thinkers and to make demands on the television hegemonic strata for positive imageries. This can be a synergetic response from the viewers. Also, educators can help individuals to believe that they can make a difference and to feel self-empowered. This feeling of self-empowerment will help the individuals to function as effective catalyzers who know that they can forcefully challenge the television hegemonic strata.

If the television hegemonic strata do not cooperate, then the catalyzers can discontinue their financial and viewing support of all the entities that comprise the television industry.

The Change Agent as Process Helper. Again, sponsors/ educators can utilize their skills to make the viewers aware of the negative television imageries. These sponsors are process helpers who implement changes within the television industry when the viewers declare that the television hegemonic strata must develop and film positive television imageries or risk the lack of financial and viewing support from the viewers. Therefore, the viewers *and* the sponsors function as change agents.

The Change Agent as Solution Giver. A solution giver "creates awareness of the solution's value and to gain its ultimate acceptance." Because the television industry uses airwaves that legally belong to the public, the public should be fairly and justly represented on television. The solution giver can make the members of the television industry aware of the fact that television should be utilized as an educational instrument that may form for people, positive self-perceptions and positive perceptions of other cultural people. Thereafter, television can be responsible for helping to effectuate a racially and sexually balanced society. Only then will the television industry rightfully serve the public whose airwaves are being used by the television industry.

The Change Agent as Resource Linker. Havelock (1973) states that resources are inclusive of "special knowledge; . . . the ability to formulate and adapt solutions; or expertise in the process of change." Pertaining to shaping positive imageries of African-Americans, the change agents can be skillful African-American writers, directors, producers, and actors who wish to construct positive imageries of African-Americans. Those change agents can empower themselves by not compromising their expertise and integrity in exchange for monetary rewards from the television hegemonic strata. Instead, the change agents can individually or synergistically finance and fashion positive African-American imageries that can be aired on public television or a cable channel that is committed to perpetuating positive imageries of African-Americans.

Notwithstanding, if the television hegemonic strata wish to hire any of the change agents, the agents can be invaluable resource linkers because of their special knowledge about African-American imageries, their knowledge about adapting solutions relative to negative imageries of African-Americans, and their expertise in the process of these changes.

Finally, I consider myself to be a change agent. My commitment is to help improve the human condition of young adult African-Americans by financing and producing records, videos, and films which will reflect the rich cultural diversity of African-Americans. Hopefully, this commitment will cast positive conceptual and perceptual changes to counter the predominate negative television imageries of African-Americans.

CONCLUSION

In this study, I asked several questions to elicit thoughts and feelings about the African-American young adults' perceptions pertaining to the nineteen television episodes. However, when African-American young adults are watching television, without being questioned about the imageries, they might not be analytical about the imageries; that is, the young adults might not have the skills to peel away the layers of the imageries' messages. Because of this, television viewers should not support the television hegemonic strata's television shows that perpetuate negative imageries of African-Americans. Besides being devastating and demeaning for African-Americans, the negative television imageries of African-Americans are eternalized on film for the world's populace to see.

Young African-Americans, as well as older African-Americans, should not allow "others" to define African-Americans. African-Americans are heterogeneous people whose self-definition and heterogeneity are rarely manifested on television shows. Instead, I think that negative group attribution pertaining to African-Americans is repeatedly supported on television shows.

As cited in Chapter II, Postman (1982) said, "People watch television, not read it. It is the picture that dominates the viewers' consciousness. . . . Watching television requires instantaneous pattern-recognition, not delayed analytic decoding." It is inexcusable for the powerful, influential, television hegemonic strata to ignore the prodigious political, educational, community, inventive, artistic, and family histories of African-American people. It is outrageous that, since the beginning of the twentieth century, the television hegemonic strata spent phenomenal time and money to create, produce, and film humiliating, confirming imageries of African-Americans.

However, despite its history, television can become an educational instrument to teach egalitarian principles to the populace of America and the world. The challenge that the television industry must face is to become a true educational tool, that is, an entity that acknowledges that its fundamental responsibility to all young people is to help them realize their capabilities and goals. The television industry must join the effort to make education a more positive and powerful means for equality in our democracy.

Appendix A

Nielsen Media Research

Hours of TV Usage

Blacks continued to watch more TV than All Other households, according to Nielsen Media Research. November's average weekly viewing figure of 72 hours in Black homes - compared to 48 hours 12 minutes in All Other homes - was the highest of the other 1989-1990 broadcast months reported here. July's Black average viewing level of 65 hours 24 minutes was the lowest of the four periods.

Viewing among Black households held steady in Primetime during November and February at 14 hours 36 minutes before decreasing slightly to 13 hours 48 minutes in May and 12 hours 54 minutes in July. Primetime viewing among All Other households peaked in February (12 hours 48 minutes) followed by November (12 hours 36 minutes), May (11 hours 42 minutes) and July (10 hours 30 minutes). Daytime Black viewing peaked in November (13 hours 30 minutes) while All Other peaked in July (8 hours 24 minutes).

To help analyze viewing level differences in the two groups, a Black/All Other index appears below each of the bar graphs. The index is calculated by dividing Black viewing by All Other viewing. An index of 100 indicates no difference; greater than 100 means Black viewing was higher than All Other; less than 100 means All Other viewing was higher than Black. For convenience, these indices appear throughout this report.

Chart 2
TV Usage Per Household Per Week: Avg. Hours:Minutes

☐ Mon-Sun 8:00-11:00PM
☐ Mon-Fri 10:00AM-4:30PM
▨ Remainder
Composite - a combination of Black and all other households

November 1989: (Nielsen Media Research)

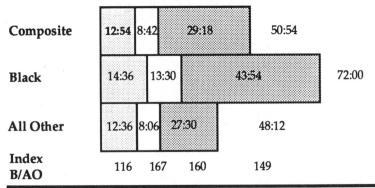

Composite	12:54	8:42	29:18	50:54
Black	14:36	13:30	43:54	72:00
All Other	12:36	8:06	27:30	48:12
Index B/AO	116	167	160	149

Chart 2 (continued)

February 1990:: (Nielsen Media Research)

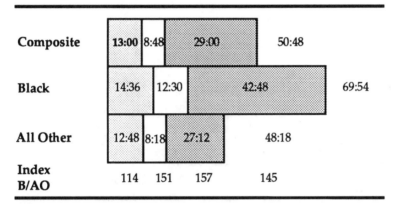

Composite	13:00	8:48	29:00	50:48
Black	14:36	12:30	42:48	69:54
All Other	12:48	8:18	27:12	48:18
Index B/AO	114	151	157	145

May 1990: (Nielsen Media Research)

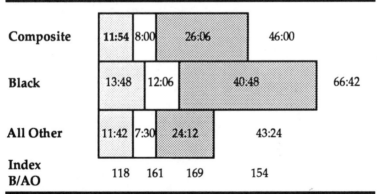

Composite	11:54	8:00	26:06	46:00
Black	13:48	12:06	40:48	66:42
All Other	11:42	7:30	24:12	43:24
Index B/AO	118	161	169	154

Chart 2 (continued)

July 1990: (Nielsen Media Research)

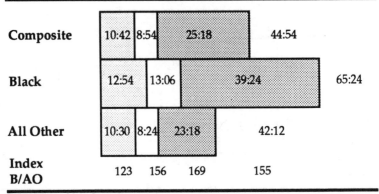

Composite	10:42	8:54	25:18	44:54
Black	12:54	13:06	39:24	65:24
All Other	10:30	8:24	23:18	42:12
Index B/AO	123	156	169	155

APPENDIX B

JUDGES' RESPONSE SHEET

JUDGES' RESPONSE SHEET

INSTRUCTIONS

Each show contains approximately five episodes. After each episode, stop the show and identify the positive and/or negative imageries that may influence the self-concept of African-American young adults.

Next, for each image that you identify, write an analysis that explains how the positive and/or negative imageries may influence self-concept.

Name of Judge: _____

Show Number: _____

Air Date: _____

Number of Episode: _____

This show has _____ episodes.

Negative Imageries	Likely Influence on Self-Concept

Show Number: _____

Episode Number: _____

Positive Imageries	Likely Influence on Self-Concept

Show Number: _____

Episode Number: _____

APPENDIX C

PERSONAL HISTORY FORM AND PROFILES OF INTERVIEWEES

PERSONAL HISTORY FORM

Year of Birth: _____

Sex: Female: _____   Male: _____

Age: _____

City and State of Residence: _____

1. What is your present occupation?   _____

2. Is your income:

    _____   Under $10,000
    _____   Between $10,000-$25,000
    _____   Between $25,000-$50,000
    _____   Between $50,000-$100,000
    _____   Above $100,000

3. Do you own your home?   _____

4. What is/are your education experience/experiences?
    (More than one may be checked, if applicable)

    _____   Completed High School
    _____   High School Diploma
    _____   Attended, but not completed college
    _____   Associate's Degree
    _____   Undergraduate College Degree
    _____   Vocational School Degree
    _____   Graduate Degree
    _____   More than one graduate degree

PROFILES OF INTERVIEWEES

Thelma:

Thelma, eighteen years old, is a college freshman. She works as a clerk, earning an income of less than $10,000 per year; and she aspires to be a correctional officer.

Lisa:

Lisa, twenty-five years old, is a college graduate. She works as a secretary, earning an income between $10,000 and $25,000 per year.

Barbara:

Barbara, twenty-five years old, is a college graduate. She is a fashion designer who earns between $25,000 and $50,000 per year.

Elizabeth:

Elizabeth, twenty-four years old, is a college graduate who is currently a third-year law student. She earns between $10,000 and $25,000 per year.

Ahmed:

Ahmed, twenty-four years old, is a college graduate. He is an electrical engineer who earns between $25,000 and $50,000 per year.

Keri:

Keri, twenty-two years old, is a high school graduate. She attended college but did not obtain a degree. Presently, Keri is a school substitute vocational assistant who earns between $10,000 and $25,000 per year.

Leroy:

Leroy, twenty-five years old, is a college graduate. Currently, he is unemployed.

John:

John, twenty-three years old, is a high school graduate. He is attending college and earns less than $10,000 per year.

Gordon:

Gordon, nineteen years old, is a college student. His income is less than $10,000.

David:

David, twenty-three years old, is a high school graduate. He has attended college, but he did not obtain a degree. He is currently employed, earning a salary that is under $10,000 per year.

BIBLIOGRAPHY

GENERAL REFERENCES

Ebony Magazine Editors. (1971, 1974). *Ebony pictorial history of Black America: African past to the Civil War.* Volume I. Chicago, IL: Johnson Publishing Company, Inc.

Havelock, R. G. (1973). *The change agent's guide to innovation in education.* Englewood Cliffs, NJ: Educational Technology Publications.

Patton, M. Q. (1991). *Strategic themes in qualitative methods, qualitative evaluation, and research methods.* Newbury Park, CA: Sage Publications.

Pfeiffer, J. W., & Ballew, A. C. (Eds.). *Theories and models in applied behavioral science.* Volume 4. San Diego, CA: Pfeiffer and Company.

INFLUENCE OF PERCEPTION ON HUMAN BEHAVIOR

Allport, G. W. (1954). *The nature of prejudice.* Cambridge, MA: Addison-Wesley Publishing Company.

Bagley, C., Verma, G., Mallick, K., & Young, L. (1979). *Personality, self-esteem, and prejudice.* England: Saxon House.

Banks, J. A. (1972). "Racial prejudice and the Black self-concept." In J. A. Banks & J. D. Grambs (Eds.), *Black self-concept* (pp. 7-8). New York: McGraw-Hill Book Company.

Berscheid, R., & Walster, E. (1974). "Physical attractiveness." In L. Berkowitz (Ed.), *Advances in experimental social psychology*, Volume 7. New York: Academic Press.

Cacioppo, J. T., Harkins, S. G., & Petty, R. (1981). "The nature of attitudes and cognitive responses and their relationship to behavior." In R. C. Petty, T. M. Ostrom, & T. C. Brock (Eds.), *Cognitive responses in persuasion*. Hillsdale, NJ: Erlbaum.

Clark, K. B. (1955). *Prejudice and your child*. Boston, MA: The Beacon Press.

Clark, K., & Clark, M. (1950). "Emotional factors in racial identification and reference in Negro children." *Journal of Negro Education*, 341-350.

Clarke, J. H. (1990). *Can African people save themselves?* Michigan: Alkebulans.

Daniel, J. H. (1992, February 20). Personal communication.

Dennis, R. M. (1981). "Socialization and racism: The White experience." In B. P. Bowser & R. G. Hunt (Eds.), *Impacts of racism on White Americans* (p. 73). Newbury Park, CA: Sage Publications.

Duncan, B. L. (1976). "Differential social perceptions and the attribution of intergroup violence: Testing the lower limits of stereotyping of Blacks." *Journal of Personality and Social Psychology, 34*, 590-598.

Ehrlich, H. J. (1973). "The social psychology of prejudice." *Personality, self-esteem, and prejudice*. New York: John Wiley.

Erikson, E. (1968). *Identity, youth, and crisis*. New York: W. W. Norton.

Fishbein, M., & Ajzen, J. (1981). "Acceptance, yielding, and impact: Cognitive processes in persuasion." In R. C. Petty, T. M. Ostrom, & T. C. Brock (Eds.), *Cognitive responses in persuasion* (p. 340). Hillsdale, CA: Erlbaum.

Goffman, C. (1959). *The presentation of self in everyday life.* Garden City, NJ: Doubleday.

Granberg, D. (1984). "Attributing attitudes to members of groups." In J. R. Eiser (Ed.), *Attitudinal judgement.* New York: Springer Publishing Company.

Gurwitz, S. B., & Dodge, K. A. (1977). "Effects of confirmations and disconfirmations on stereotype based attributions." *The Journal of Personality and Social Psychology, 33,* 499.

Hamilton, D. L. (1979). "A cognitive attributional analysis of stereotyping." In L. Berkowitz (Ed.), *Advances in experimental social psychology,* Volume 2. New York: Academic Press.

Hamilton, D. L. (1981). "Cognitive processes in stereotyping and intergroup behavior." In S. E. Taylor (Ed.), *Cognitive processes of stereotyping and intergroup behavior.* Hillsdale, NJ: Erlbaum.

Hamilton, D. L., & Rose, T. L. (1980). "Illusory correlation and the maintenance of stereotypic belief." *Journal of Personality and Social Psychology, 39*(5), 833-834.

Howard, J., & Rothbart, M. (1980). "Social categorization and memory for in-group and out-group behavior." *Journal of Personality and Social Psychology, 38,* 301-310.

Huges, J., & Demo, D. H. (1981). *Human groups and social categories.* New York: Cambridge University Press.

Huges, J., & Demo, D. H. (1989). *Self-perceptions of Black Americans: Self-esteem and personal efficacy*. Chicago, IL: University of Chicago Press.

Kelly, G. A. (1955). *The psychology of personal constructs*. New York: W. W. Norton.

Moynihan, D. P. (1966, 1967). *The Moynihan Report*. Washington, D. C.: U. S. Department of Labor.

Norton, D. (1983). "Black family life patterns, the development of self, and cognitive development of Black children." In G. Johnson Powell (Ed.), *The psychosocial development of minority group children*. New York: Brunner/Mazel.

Poussaint, A. F. (1974, August): "Building a strong self-image in Black children." *Ebony Magazine*, 138-143.

Rogers, C. (1989). *Carl Rogers--Dialogue: Conversations with Martin Buber, Paul Tillich, B. S. Skinner, Gregory Bateson, Michael Polanyi, Rollo May, and Others*. Howard Kirschenbaum & Valerie Land Henderson (Eds.). Boston: Houghton Mifflin.

Rokeach, M. (1973). *The nature of human values*. New York: Free Press.

Rosenbert, M., & Simmon, R. (1972). *Black and White self-esteem: The urban school child*. Washington, D. C.: The American Sociological Association.

Rothstein, M. (1991, August 14). "From cartoons to a play about racism in the 60's." *The New York Times*, p. 11, Section C.

Sherif, M., & Sherif, C. (1967). *Groups in harmony and tension*. New York: Harper.

Snyder, M., Tanke, E., & Berscheid, E. (1977). *Journal of Personality and Social Psychology, 35*(9), 658-659.

Syngg, D., & Coombs, A. (1949). *Individual behavior.* New York: Harper.

Tajfel, H., (1981). *Human Group and Social Categories.* Cambridge: Cambridge University Press: 1981

Tajfel, H., & Wilkes, A. (1963). "Classification and quantitative judgement." *British Journal of Social Psychology, 54,* 101-114.

Taylor, S. E. (1981). "A categorization approach to stereotyping." In D. L. Hamilton (Ed.), *Cognitive processes in stereotyping and intergroup behavior* (pp. 86-87). Hillsdale, NJ: Erlbaum.

Taylor, S. E., Fiske, S. I., Etcoff, N. L., & Ruderman, A. F. (1978). "Categorical and contextual basis of person memory and stereotyping." *Journal of Personality and Social Psychology, 35,* 778-793.

Van Dijk, A. (1987). *Communicating racism: Ethnic prejudice in thought and talk.* London/New Delhi: Sage Publications.

Weber, R., & Crocker, J. (1983). "Cognitive processes in the revision of stereotypic beliefs." *Journal of Personality and Social Psychology, 45*(5).

Webster, Merriam. (1976). *Webster's third new international dictionary of the English language unabridged.* Springfield, MA: Merriam-Webster Inc., Publishers.

Wilder, D. A. (1981). "Perceiving persons as a group: Categorization and intergroup relations." In D. L. Hamilton (Ed.), *Cognitive processes in stereotyping and intergroup behavior.* Hillsdale, NJ: Erlbaum.

Woodruff, A. D. (1942). "Personal values and the direction of behavior." *School Review*, 33.

Young, K., & Mack, R. (1962). *Systematic sociology*. New York: American Book.

IMPACT OF TELEVISION IMAGERIES ON SELF-PERCEPTIONS

Barnes, E. J. (1980). "The Black community as the source of positive self-concept for Black children: A theoretical perspective." In R. L. Jones (Ed.), *Black psychology*. New York: Harper & Row Publishers, Inc.

Bogle, D. (1988). *Blacks in American films and television: An encyclopedia*. New York: Fireside.

Bogle, D. (1989). *Toms, coons, mulattos, mammies, and bucks*. New York: Continuum Publishing.

Comstock, G., Chaffee, S., Katzman, N., McCombs, M., & Roberts, D. (1978). *Television and human behavior*. New York: Columbia University Press.

Dates, J. L. (1990). "Commercial television." In J. L. Dates & W. Barlow (Eds.), *Split image: African-Americans in the mass media*. Washington, D. C.: Howard University Press.

Fishbein, M., & Ajzen, I. (1981). "Acceptance, yielding, and impact: Cognitive processes in persuasion." In R. C. Petty, T. M. Ostrom, & T. C. Brock (Eds.), *Cognitive responses in persuasion*. Hillsdale, NJ: Erlbaum.

Greenfield, P., & Beagles-Roos, J. (1988). "Radio vs. television: Their cognitive impact on children of different socioeconomic and ethnic groups." *Journal of Communication*, 38(2).

Gerbner, G., & Gross, J. (1976). "Living with television: The violence profile." *Journal of Communication, 76,* 182-190.

Hawkins, R., & Pingree, S. (1980). "Some processes in the cultivation effort." *Communication Research, 7*(2), 195-226. London/New Delhi: Sage Publications.

Huston, A. C., Donnerstein, E., Fairchild, H., Feshbach, N. D., Katz, P. A., Murray, J. P., Rubinstein, E. A., Wilcox, B. L., & Zuckerman, D. (1992). *The role of television in American society: Big world, small screen.* Lincoln, NE: University of Nebraska Press.

Klapper, T. T. (1954). "The comparative effects of the various media." In W. Schramm (Ed.), *The process and effects of mass communication.* Urbana, IL: University of Illinois.

Kunjufu, J. (1984). *Developing positive self-images and discipline in Black children.* Chicago, IL: African-American Images.

Lee, M. A., & Solomon, N. (1990). *Unreliable sources: A guide to directing bias in news media.* New York: Carol Publishing Group.

Mander, J. (1978). *Arguments for the elimination of television.* New York: Quill.

McLeod, J. M., Atkins, C. K., & Chaffee, S. H. (1972). "Adolescents, parents, and television use: Adolescent self-report measures from Maryland and Wisconsin samples." *Television and social behavior,* Volume 3. Washington, D. C.: U. S. Government Printing Office.

Nisbett, R. E., & Ross, L. (1980). *Human inferences: Strategies and shortcomings of social judgement.* Englewood Cliffs, NJ: Prentice-Hall Inc.

O'Connor, J. J. (1991, June 9). No laugh track, no deal. *The New York Times*, 1, Section 2.

Osborn, D. K., & Endsley, R. C. (1971). "Emotional reactions to young children to T. V. violence." *Child Development, 42.*

Postman, N. (1982). *The disappearance of childhood.* New York: Delacorte Press.

Radecki, T. (1991, July 23). "Fight against T. V. and movie violence." *U.S.A. Today,* 10, Section A.

Reddick, L. (1975). "In Black films and filmmakers: A comprehensive anthology from stereotype to superhero." In L. Patterson (Ed.), *Of motion pictures.* New York: Dodd, Mead.

Robinson, D. (1991, September 28). "Have Blacks passed the screen test?" *The Times,* 12.

Sinclair, A. (1991, September 21, 28). "The Hollywood connection." *The New York Amsterdam News,* 28.

Steinfeld, J. L. (1973, April). "T. V. violence is harmful." *Reader's Digest,* 37-45.

Sutton, P. E. (1989, September 15). *Minority ownership as a method of increasing diversity in programming.* Presentation to the U. S. Senate Communications Subcommittee.

Tan, A. S., & Tan, G. (1979). "Television use and self-esteem of Blacks." *Journal of Communication, 29* (1).

Warren, N. (1988). "From Uncle Tom to Cliff Huxtable, Aunt Jemima to Aunt Nell: Images of Blacks in film and the television industry." In J. C. Smith (Ed.), *Images of Blacks in American culture: A reference guide to information sources.* Westport, CT: Greenwood Press.

INDEX